Modern Critical Interpretations

Joseph Conrad's Heart of Darkness

Modern Critical Interpretations

These and other titles in preparation

Joseph Conrad's
Heart of Darkness

Edited and with an introduction by
Harold Bloom
Sterling Professor of the Humanities
Yale University

Chelsea House Publishers
NEW YORK ◇ PHILADELPHIA

© 1987 by Chelsea House Publishers, a division
of Main Line Book Co.

Introduction © 1986 by Harold Bloom

Printed and bound in the United States of America

10   9   8   7

∞ The paper used in this publication meets the minimum
requirements of the American National Standard for Permanence
of Paper for Printed Library Materials, Z39.48-1984.

Library of Congress Cataloging-in-Publication Data
Joseph Conrad's Heart of darkness.
    (Modern critical interpretations)
    Bibliography: p.
    Includes index.
    1. Conrad, Joseph, 1857–1924. Heart of darkness.
I. Bloom, Harold, 1930–   . II. Series.
PR6005.04H477   1987   823'.912   86-21600
ISBN 1-55546-015-1

Contents

Editor's Note

This book brings together what seems to me the best criticism available upon Joseph Conrad's famous and problematic short novel, *Heart of Darkness,* one of the novelist's most widely read and influential works. I am grateful to David Parker for his aid in researching this volume.

The essays are reprinted here in the chronological order of their original publication. My introduction broods upon what could be called the obscurantism of *Heart of Darkness,* its curious referential indefiniteness which doubtless universalizes its appeal, but perhaps at the cost of its final coherence.

Albert J. Guerard begins the chronological sequence of criticism by charting the book as "a *Pilgrim's Progress* for our pessimistic and psychologizing age." In contrast, James Guetti sees in the short novel's journey to the center "the refutation of such a journey," since no meaning can be found at the center. C. B. Cox more amiably finds meaning in a possible "choice of nightmares" offered by the narrative, while Bruce Henricksen evokes ancient Gnostic myth, with its repudiation of inwardness as demonism, as a proper context for Conrad's story.

In a very different interpretation from any of these, R. A. Gekoski concludes that Conrad judges the truth to be unendurable, and so subtly insinuates that the reader should solace herself with a saving illusion. Usefully invoking the context of ninteteenth-century thought, Ian Watt nevertheless finds in *Heart of Darkness* presages of Sartre and Camus. In a parallel investigation, John Tessitore attempts a modified Freudian reading of the book, with considerable additional references to Dostoyevski's Underground Man.

A more sophisticated Freudian interpretation, informed also by contemporary advanced theories of narrative, is given by Peter

Brooks, who finds in the short novel's emphasis upon repetition a deep analogue with Freud's *Beyond the Pleasure Principle*. Another contemporary reading, indebted to Bakhtin's work on Rabelais, is ventured by Aaron Fogel, who concludes this book by shrewdly noting both Conrad's fear that he resembled Kurtz, and Conrad's saving difference from his fated hero–villain.

Introduction

I

In Conrad's "Youth" (1898), Marlow gives us a brilliant description of the sinking of the *Judea*:

> "Between the darkness of earth and heaven she was burning fiercely upon a disc of purple sea shot by the blood-red play of gleams; upon a disc of water glittering and sinister. A high, clear flame, an immense and lonely flame, ascended from the ocean, and from its summit the black smoke poured continuously at the sky. She burned furiously; mournful and imposing like a funeral pile kindled in the night, surrounded by the sea, watched over by the stars. A magnificent death had come like a grace, like a gift, like a reward to that old ship at the end of her laborious day. The surrender of her weary ghost to the keeper of the stars and sea was stirring like the sight of a glorious triumph. The masts fell just before daybreak, and for a moment there was a burst and turmoil of sparks that seemed to fill with flying fire the night patient and watchful, the vast night lying silent upon the sea. At daylight she was only a charred shell, floating still under a cloud of smoke and bearing a glowing mass of coal within.
>
> "Then the oars were got out, and the boats forming in a line moved around her remains as if in procession—the longboat leading. As we pulled across her stern a slim dart of fire shot out viciously at us, and suddenly she went down, head first, in a great hiss of steam. The unconsumed stern was the last to sink; but the paint had gone, had cracked, had peeled off, and there were no letters,

1

there was no word, no stubborn device that was like her soul, to flash at the rising sun her creed and her name."

The apocalyptic vividness is enhanced by the visual nameless-ness of the "unconsumed stern," as though the creed of Christ's people maintained both its traditional refusal to violate the Second Commandment, and its traditional affirmation of its not-to-be-named God. With the *Judea,* Conrad sinks the romance of youth's illusions, but like all losses in Conrad this submersion in the destruc-tive element is curiously dialectical, since only experiential loss al-lows for the compensation of an imaginative gain in the represen-tation of artistic truth. Originally the ephebe of Flaubert and of Flaubert's "son," Maupassant, Conrad was reborn as the narrative disciple of Henry James, the James of *The Spoils of Poynton* and *What Maisie Knew,* rather than the James of the final phase.

Ian Watt convincingly traces the genesis of Marlow to the way that "James developed the indirect narrative approach through the sensitive central intelligence of one of the characters." Marlow, whom James derided as "that preposterous magic mariner," actually represents Conrad's swerve away from the excessive strength of James's influence upon him. By always "mixing himself up with the narrative," in James's words. Marlow guarantees an enigmatic re-serve that increases the distance between the impressionistic tech-niques of Conrad and James. Though there is little valid comparison that can be made between Conrad's greatest achievements and the hesitant, barely fictional status of Pater's *Marius the Epicurean,* Con-rad's impressionism is as extreme and solipsistic as Pater's. There is a definite parallel between the fates of Sebastian Van Storck (in Pa-ter's *Imaginary Portraits*) and Decoud in *Nostromo.*

In his 1897 "Preface" to *The Nigger of the "Narcissus,"* Conrad famously insisted that his creative task was "before all to make you *see.*" He presumably was aware that he thus joined himself to a line of prose seers whose latest representatives were Carlyle, Ruskin, and Pater. There is a movement in that group from Carlyle's exuberant "Natural Supernaturalism" through Ruskin's paganization of Evan-gelical fervor to Pater's evasive and skeptical Epicurean materialism, with its eloquent suggestion that all we can see is the flux of sensa-tions. Conrad exceeds Pater in the reduction of impressionism to a state of consciousness where the seeing narrator is hopelessly mixed up with the seen narrative. James may seem an impressionist when compared to Flaubert, but alongside of Conrad he is clearly shown to be a kind of Platonist, imposing forms and resolutions upon the flux of human relations by an exquisite formal geometry altogether his own.

To observe that Conrad is metaphysically less of an idealist is hardly to argue that he is necessarily a stronger novelist than his master, James. It may suggest though that Conrad's originality is more disturbing than that of James, and may help explain why Conrad, rather than James, became the dominant influence upon the generation of American novelists that included Hemingway, Fitzgerald, and Faulkner. The cosmos of *The Sun Also Rises, The Great Gatsby,* and *As I Lay Dying* derives from *Heart of Darkness* and *Nostromo* rather than from *The Ambassadors* and *The Golden Bowl.* Darl Bundren is the extreme inheritor of Conrad's quest to carry impressionism into its heart of darkness in the human awareness that we are only a flux of sensations gazing outwards upon a flux of impressions.

II

Heart of Darkness may always be a critical battleground between readers who regard it as an aesthetic triumph, and those like myself who doubt its ability to rescue us from its own hopeless obscurantism. That Marlow seems, at moments, not to know what he is talking about, is almost certainly one of the narrative's deliberate strengths, but if Conrad also seems finally not to know, then he necessarily loses some of his authority as a storyteller. Perhaps he loses it to death—our death, or our anxiety that he will not sustain the illusion of his fiction's duration long enough for us to sublimate the frustrations it brings us.

These frustrations need not be deprecated. Conrad's diction, normally flawless, is notoriously vague throughout *Heart of Darkness.* E. M. Forster's wicked comment on Conrad's entire work is justified perhaps only when applied to *Heart of Darkness:*

> Misty in the middle as well as at the edges, the secret cask
> of his genius contains a vapour rather than a jewel. . . .
> No creed, in fact.

Forster's misty vapor seems to inhabit such Conradian recurrent modifiers as "monstrous," "unspeakable," "atrocious," and many more, but these are minor defects compared to the involuntary self-parody that Conrad inflicts upon himself. There are moments that sound more like James Thurber lovingly satirizing Conrad than like Conrad:

> We had carried Kurtz into the pilot house: there was more air there. Lying on the couch, he stared through the open shutter. There was an eddy in the mass of human bodies, and the woman with helmeted head and tawny cheeks rushed out to the very brink of the stream. She put out her hands, shouted something, and all that wild mob took up the shout in a roaring chorus of articulated, rapid, breathless utterance.
>
> "Do you understand this?" I asked.
>
> He kept on looking out past me with fiery, longing eyes, with a mingled expression of wistfulness and hate. He made no answer, but I saw a smile, a smile of indefinable meaning, appear on his colorless lips that a moment after twitched convulsively. "Do I not?" he said slowly, gasping, as if the words had been torn out of him by a supernatural power.

This cannot be defended as an instance of what Frank Kermode calls a language "needed when Marlow is not equal to the experience described." Has the experience been described here? Smiles of "indefinable meaning" are smiled once too often in a literary text if they are smiled even once. *Heart of Darkness* has taken on some of the power of myth, even if the book is limited by its involuntary obscurantism. It has haunted American literature from T. S. Eliot's poetry through our major novelists of the era 1920 to 1940, on to a line of movies that go from the *Citizen Kane* of Orson Welles (a substitute for an abandoned Welles project to film *Heart of Darkness*) on to Coppola's *Apocalypse Now*. In this instance, Conrad's formlessness seems to have worked as an aid, so diffusing his conception as to have made it available to an almost universal audience.

"the flabby devil" of the Central Station. Later, when he discovers what has happened to Kurtz's moral ideas, he remains faithful to the "nightmare of my choice." In *Under Western Eyes* Sophia Antonovna makes a distinction between those who burn and those who rot, and remarks that it is sometimes preferable to burn. The Kurtz who had made himself literally one of the devils of the land, and who in solitude had kicked himself loose of the earth, burns while the others rot. Through violent not flabby evil he exists in the moral universe even before pronouncing judgment on himself with his dying breath. A little too much has been made, I think, of the redemptive value of those two words—"The horror!" But none of the company "pilgrims" could have uttered them.

The redemptive view is Catholic, of course, though no priest was in attendance; Kurtz can repent as the gunman of *The Power and the Glory* cannot. *Heart of Darkness* (still at this public and wholly conscious level) combines a Victorian ethic and late Victorian fear of the white man's deterioration with a distinctly Catholic psychology. We are protected from ourselves by society with its laws and its watchful neighbors, Marlow observes. And we are protected by work. "You wonder I didn't go ashore for a howl and a dance? Well, no—I didn't. Fine sentiments, you say? Fine sentiments, be hanged! I had no time. I had to mess about with white-lead and strips of woolen blanket helping to put bandages on those leaky steam-pipes." But when the external restraints of society and work are removed, we must meet the challenge and temptation of savage reversion with our "own inborn strength. Principles won't do." This inborn strength appears to include restraint—the restraint that Kurtz lacked and the cannibal crew of the *Roi des Belges* surprisingly possessed. The hollow man, whose evil is the evil of *vacancy,* succumbs. And in their different degrees the pilgrims and Kurtz share this hollowness. "Perhaps there was nothing within" the manager of the Central Station. "Such a suspicion made one pause—for out there there were no external checks." And there was nothing inside the brickmaker, that papier-mâché Mephistopheles, "but a little loose dirt, maybe."

As for Kurtz, the wilderness "echoed loudly within him because he was hollow at the core." Perhaps the chief contradiction of *Heart of Darkness* is that it suggests and dramatizes evil as an active energy (Kurtz and his unspeakable lusts) but defines evil as vacancy. The primitive (and here the contradiction is only verbal) is compact of passion and apathy.. "I was struck by the fire of his eyes and the composed languor of his expression. This shadow looked satiated and calm, as though for the moment it had had its fill of all the emotions." Of the two menaces—the unspeakable desires and the apathy—apathy surely seemed the greater to Conrad. Hence we cannot quite believe the response of Marlow's heart to the beating of the tom-toms. This is, I think, the story's minor but central flaw, and the source of an unfruitful ambiguity: that it slightly overdoes the kinship with the "passionate uproar," slightly undervalues the temptation of inertia.

In any event, it is time to recognize that the story is not primarily about Kurtz or about the brutality of Belgian officials but about Marlow its narrator. To what extent it also expresses the Joseph Conrad a biographer might conceivably recover, who in 1898 still felt a debt must be paid for his Congo journey and who paid it by the writing of this story, is doubtless an insoluble question. I suspect two facts (of a possible several hundred) are important. First, that going to the Congo was the enactment of a childhood wish associated with the disapproved childhood ambition to go to sea, and that this belated enactment was itself profoundly disapproved, in 1890, by the uncle and guardian. It was another gesture of a man bent on throwing his life away. But even more important may be the guilt of complicity, just such a guilt as many novelists of the Second World War have been obliged to work off. What Conrad thought of the expedition of the Katanga Company of 1890–1892 is accurately reflected in his remarks on the "Eldorado Exploring Expedition" of *Heart of Darkness:* "It was reckless without hardihood, greedy without audacity, and cruel without courage . . . with no more moral purpose at the back of it than there is in burglars breaking into a safe." Yet Conrad hoped to obtain command of the expedition's ship even after he had returned from the initiatory voyage dramatized in his novel. Thus the adventurous Conrad and Conrad the moralist may have experienced collision. But the collision, again as with so many novelists of the second war, could well have been deferred and retrospective, not felt intensely at the time.

So much for the elusive Conrad of the biographers and of the "Congo Diary." Substantially and in its central emphasis *Heart of Darkness* concerns Marlow (projection to whatever great or small degree of a more irrecoverable Conrad) and his journey toward and through certain facets or potentialities of self. F. R. Leavis seems to regard him as a narrator only, providing a "specific and concretely realized point of view." But Marlow reiterates often enough that he is recounting a spiritual voyage of self-discovery. He remarks casually but crucially that he did not know himself before setting out, and that he likes work for the chance it provides to "find yourself . . . what no other man can ever know." The Inner Station "was the farthest point of navigation and the culminating point of my experience." At a material and rather superficial level, the journey is through the temptation of atavism. It is a record of "remote kinship" with the "wild and passionate uproar," of a "trace of a response" to it, of a final rejection of the "fascination of the abomination." And why should there not be the trace of a response? "The mind of man is capable of anything—because everything is in it, all the past as well as all the future." Marlow's temptation is made concrete through his exposure to Kurtz, a white man and sometime idealist who had fully responded to the wilderness: a potential and fallen self. "I had turned to the wilderness really, not to Mr. Kurtz." At the climax Marlow follows Kurtz ashore, confounds the beat of the drum with the beating of his heart, goes through the ordeal of looking into Kurtz's "mad soul," and brings him back to the ship. He returns to Europe a changed and more knowing man. Ordinary people are now "intruders whose knowledge of life was to me an irritating pretence, because I felt so sure they could not possibly know the things I knew."

On this literal plane, and when the events are so abstracted from the dream-sensation conveying them, it is hard to take Marlow's plight very seriously. Will he, the busy captain and moralizing narrator, also revert to savagery, go ashore for a howl and a dance, indulge unspeakable lusts? The late Victorian reader (and possibly Conrad himself) could take this more seriously than we; could literally believe not merely in Kurtz's deterioration through months of solitude but also in the sudden reversions to the "beast" of naturalistic fiction. Insofar as Conrad does want us to take it seriously and literally, we must admit the nominal triumph of a currently accepted but false psychology over his own truer intuitions. But the triumph is only nominal. For the personal narrative is unmistakably authentic, which means that it explores something truer, more fundamental, and distinctly less material: the night journey into the unconscious, and confrontation of an entity within the self. "I flung one shoe overboard, and became aware that that was exactly what I had been looking forward to—a talk with Kurtz." It little matters what, in terms of psychological symbolism, we call this double or say he represents: whether the Freudian id or the Jungian shadow or more vaguely the outlaw. And I am afraid it is impossible to say where Conrad's conscious understanding of his story began and ended. The important thing is that the introspective plunge and powerful dream seem true; and are therefore inevitably moving.

Certain circumstances of Marlow's voyage, looked at in these terms, take on a new importance. The true night journey can occur (except during analysis) only in sleep or in the waking dream of a profoundly intuitive mind. Marlow insists more than is necessary on the dreamlike quality of his narrative. "It seems to me I am trying to tell you a dream—making a vain attempt, because no relation of a dream can convey the dream-sensation, that commingling of absurdity, surprise, and bewilderment in a tremor of struggling revolt." Even before leaving Brussels Marlow felt as though he "were about to set off for the center of the earth," not the center of a continent. The introspective voyager leaves his familiar rational world, is "cut off from the comprehension" of his surroundings; his steamer toils "along slowly on the edge of a black and incomprehensible frenzy." As the crisis approaches, the dreamer and his ship move through a silence that "seemed unnatural, like a state of trance"; then enter (a few miles below the Inner Station) a deep fog. "The approach to this Kurtz grubbing for ivory in the wretched bush was beset by as many dangers as though he had been an enchanted princess sleeping in a fabulous castle." Later, Marlow's task is to try "to break the spell" of the wilderness that holds Kurtz entranced.

The approach to the unconscious and primitive may be aided by a savage or half-savage guide, and may require the token removal of civilized trappings or aids; both conceptions are beautifully dramatized in Faulkner's "The Bear." In *Heart of Darkness* the token "relinquishment" and the death of the half-savage guide are connected. The helmsman falling at Marlow's feet casts blood on his shoes, which he is "morbidly anxious" to change and in fact throws overboard. (The rescue of Wait in *The Nigger of the "Narcissus"* shows a similar pattern.) Here we have presumably entered an area of unconscious creation; the dream is true but the teller may have no idea why it is. So too, possibly, a psychic need as well as literary tact compelled Conrad to defer the meeting between Marlow and Kurtz for some three thousand words after announcing that it took place. We think we are about to meet Kurtz at last. But instead Marlow leaps ahead to his meeting with the Intended; comments on Kurtz's megalomania and assumption of his place among the devils of the land; reports on the seventeen-page pamphlet; relates his meeting and conversation with Kurtz's harlequin disciple—and only then tells of seeing through his binoculars the heads on the stakes surrounding Kurtz's house. This is the "evasive" Conrad in full play, deferring what we most want to know and see; perhaps compelled to defer climax in this way. The tactic is dramatically effective, though possibly carried to excess: we are told on the authority of completed knowledge certain things we would have found hard to believe had they been presented through a slow consecutive realistic discovery. But also it can be argued that it was psychologically impossible for Marlow to go at once to Kurtz's house with the others. The double must be brought on board the ship, and the first confrontation must occur there. We are reminded of Leggatt in the narrator's cabin, of the trapped Wait on the *Narcissus*. The incorporation and alliance between the two becomes material, and the identification of "selves."

Hence the shock Marlow experiences when he discovers that Kurtz's cabin is empty and his secret sharer gone; a part of himself has vanished. "What made this emotion so overpowering was—how shall I define it?—the moral shock I received, as if something altogether monstrous, intolerable to thought and odious to the soul, had been thrust upon me unexpectedly." And now he must risk the ultimate confrontation in a true solitude and must do so on shore. "I was anxious to deal with this shadow by myself alone—and to this day I don't know why I was so jealous of sharing with anyone the peculiar blackness of that experience." He follows the crawling Kurtz through the grass; comes upon him "long, pale, indistinct, like a vapor exhaled by the earth." ("I had cut him off cleverly.") We are told very little of what Kurtz said in the moments that follow; and little of his incoherent discourses after he is brought back to the ship. "His was an impenetrable darkness. I looked at him as you peer down at a man who is lying at the bottom of a precipice where the sun never shines"—a comment less vague and rhetorical, in terms of psychic geography, than it may seem at a first reading. And then Kurtz is dead, taken off the ship, his body buried in a "muddy hole." With the confrontation over, Marlow must still emerge from environing darkness, and does so through that other deep fog of sickness. The identification is not yet completely broken. "And it is not my own extremity I remember best—a vision of grayness without form filled with physical pain, and a careless contempt for the evanescence of all things—even of this pain itself. No! It is his extremity that I seem to have lived through." Only in the atonement of his lie to Kurtz's Intended, back in the sepulchral city, does the experience come truly to an end. "I laid the ghost of his gifts at last with a lie."

Such seems to be the content of the dream. If my summary has even a partial validity it should explain and to an extent justify some of the "adjectival and worse than supererogatory insistence" to which F. R. Leavis (who sees only the travelogue and the portrait of Kurtz) objects. I am willing to grant that the unspeakable rites and unspeakable secrets become wearisome, but the fact—at once literary and psychological—is that they must remain *unspoken*. A confrontation with such a double and facet of the unconscious cannot be reported through realistic dialogue; the conversations must remain as shadowy as the narrator's conversations with Leggatt. So too when Marlow finds it hard to define the moral shock he received on seeing the empty cabin, or when he says he doesn't know why he was jealous of sharing his experience, I think we can take him literally . . . and in a sense even be thankful for his uncertainty. The greater tautness and economy of "The Secret Sharer" comes from its larger conscious awareness of the psychological process it describes; from its more deliberate use of the double as symbol. And of the two stories I happen to prefer it. But it may be the groping, fumbling *Heart of Darkness* takes us into a deeper region of the mind. If the story is not about this deeper region, and not about Marlow himself, its length is quite indefensible. But even if one were to allow that the final section is about Kurtz (which I think simply absurd), a vivid pictorial record of his unspeakable lusts and gratifications would surely have been ludicrous. I share Mr. Leavis's admiration for the heads on the stakes. But not even Kurtz could have supported many such particulars.

"I listened on the watch for the sentence, for the word, that would give me the clue to the faint uneasiness inspired by this narrative that seemed to shape itself without human lips in the heavy night air of the river." Thus one of Marlow's listeners, the original "I" who frames the story, comments on its initial effect. He has discovered how alert one must be to the ebb and flow of Marlow's narrative, and here warns the reader. But there is no single word; not even the word *trance* will do. For the shifting play of thought and feeling and image and event is very intricate. It is not vivid detail alone, the heads on stakes or the bloody shoes; nor only the dark mass of moralizing abstraction; nor the dramatized psychological intuitions apart from their context that give *Heart of Darkness* its brooding weight. The impressionist method—one cannot leave this story without subscribing to the obvious—finds here one of its great triumphs of tone. The random movement of the nightmare is also the controlled movement of a poem, in which a quality of feeling may be stated or suggested and only much later justified. But it is justified at last.

The method is in important ways different from that of *Lord Jim,* though the short novel was written during an interval in the long one, and though Marlow speaks to us in both. For we do not have here the radical obfuscations and sudden wrenchings and violent chronological ambiguities of *Lord Jim.* Nor are we, as in *Nostromo,* at the mercy of a wayward flashlight moving rapidly in a cluttered room. *Heart of Darkness* is no such true example of spatial form. Instead the narrative advances and withdraws as in a succession of long dark waves borne by an incoming tide. The waves encroach fairly evenly on the shore, and presently a few more feet of sand have been won. But an occasional wave thrusts up unexpectedly, much farther than the others: even as far, say, as Kurtz and his Inner Station. Or, to take the other figure: the flashlight is held firmly; there are no whimsical jerkings from side to side. But now and then it is raised higher, and for a brief moment in a sudden clear light we discern enigmatic matters to be explored much later. Thus the movement of the story is sinuously progressive, with much incremental repetition. The intent is not to subject the reader to multiple strains and ambiguities, but rather to throw over him a brooding gloom, such a warm pall as those two Fates in the home office might knit, back in the sepulchral city.

Yet no figure can convey *Heart of Darkness* in all its resonance and tenebrous atmosphere. The movement is not one of penetration and withdrawal only; it is also the tracing of a large grand circle of awareness. It begins with the friends on the yacht under the dark above Gravesend and at last returns to them, to the tranquil waterway that "leading to the uttermost ends of the earth flowed sombre under an overcast sky—seemed to lead into the heart of an immense darkness." For this also "has been one of the dark places of the earth," and Marlow employs from the first his methods of reflexive reference and casual foreshadowing. The Romans were men enough to face this darkness of the Thames running between savage shores. "Here and there a military camp lost in a wilderness, like a needle in a bundle of hay—cold, fog, tempests, disease, exile, and death—death skulking in the air, in the water, in the bush." But these Romans were "no colonists," no more than the pilgrims of the Congo nineteen hundred years later; "their administration was merely a squeeze." Thus early Marlow establishes certain political values. The French gunboat firing into a continent anticipates the blind firing of the pilgrims into the jungle when the ship has been attacked. And Marlow hears of Kurtz's first attempt to emerge from the wilderness long before he meets Kurtz in the flesh, and wrestles with his reluctance to leave. Marlow returns again and again, with increasing irony, to Kurtz's benevolent pamphlet.

The travelogue as travelogue is not to be ignored; and one of Roger Casement's consular successors in the Congo (to whom I introduced *Heart of Darkness* in 1957) remarked at once that Conrad certainly had a "feel for the country." The demoralization of the first company station is rendered by a boiler "wallowing in the grass," by a railway truck with its wheels in the air. Presently Marlow will discover a scar in the hillside into which drainage pipes for the settlement had been tumbled; then will walk into the grove where the Negroes are free to die in a "greenish gloom." The sharply visualized particulars suddenly intrude on the somber intellectual flow of Marlow's meditation: magnified, arresting. The boilermaker who "had to crawl in the mud under the bottom of the steamboat . . . would tie up that beard of his in a kind of white serviette he brought for the purpose. It had loops to go over his ears." The papier-mâché Mephistopheles is as vivid, with his delicate hooked nose and glittering mica eyes. So too is Kurtz's harlequin companion and admirer, humbly dissociating himself from the master's lusts and gratifications. "I! I! I am a simple man. I have no great thoughts." And even Kurtz, shadow and symbol though he be, the man of eloquence who in this story is almost voiceless, and necessarily so—even Kurtz is sharply visualized, an "animated image of death," a skull and body emerging as from a winding sheet, "the cage of his ribs all astir, the bones of his arm waving."

This is Africa and its flabby inhabitants; Conrad did indeed have a "feel for the country." Yet the dark tonalities and final brooding impression derive as much from rhythm and rhetoric as from such visual details: derive from the high aloof ironies and from a prose that itself advances and recedes in waves. "This initiated wraith from the back of Nowhere honored me with its amazing confidence before it vanished altogether." Or, "It is strange how I accepted this unforseen partnership, this choice of nightmares forced upon me in the tenebrous land invaded by these mean and greedy phantoms." These are true Conradian rhythms, but they are also rhythms of thought. The immediate present can be rendered with great compactness and drama: the ship staggering within ten feet of the bank at the time of the attack, and Marlow's sudden glimpse of a face amongst the leaves, then of the bush "swarming with human limbs." But still more immediate and personal, it may be, are the meditative passages evoking vast tracts of time, and the "first of men taking possession of an accursed inheritance." The prose is varied, far more so than is usual in the early work, both in rhythm and in the movements from the general to the particular and back. But the shaped sentence collecting and fully expending its breath appears to be the norm. Some of the best passages begin and end with them:

> Going up that river was like traveling back to the earliest beginnings of the world, when vegetation rioted on the earth and the big trees were kings. An empty stream, a great silence, an impenetrable forest. The air was warm, thick, heavy, sluggish. There was no joy in the brilliance of sunshine. The long stretches of the waterway ran on, deserted, into the gloom of overshadowed distances. On silvery sandbanks hippos and alligators sunned themselves side by side.

The insistence on darkness, finally, and quite apart from ethical or mythical overtone, seems a right one for this extremely personal statement. There is a darkness of passivity, paralysis, immobilization; it is from the state of entranced languor rather than from the monstrous desires that the double Kurtz, this shadow, must be saved. In Freudian theory, we are told, such preoccupation may indicate fear of the feminine and passive. But may it not also be connected, through one of the spirit's multiple disguises, with a radical fear of death, that other darkness? "I had turned to the wilderness really, not to Mr. Kurtz, who, I was ready to admit, was as good as buried. And for a moment it seemed to me as if I also were buried in a vast grave full of unspeakable secrets. I felt an intolerable weight oppressing my breast, the smell of the damp earth, the unseen presence of victorious corruption, the darkness of an impenetrable night."

It would be folly to try to limit the menace of vegetation in the restless life of Conradian image and symbol. But the passage reminds us again of the story's reflexive references, and its images of deathly immobilization in grass. Most striking are the black shadows dying in the greenish gloom of the grove at the first station. But grass sprouts between the stones of the European city, a "whited sepulcher," and on the same page Marlow anticipates coming upon the remains of his predecessor: "the grass growing through his ribs was tall enough to hide his bones." The critical meeting with Kurtz occurs on a trail through the grass. Is there not perhaps an intense horror behind the casualness with which Marlow reports his discoveries, say of the Negro with the bullet in his forehead? Or: "Now and then a carrier dead in harness, at rest in the long grass near the path, with an empty water gourd and his long staff lying by his side."

All this, one must acknowledge, does not make up an ordinary light travelogue. There is no little irony in the letter of November 9, 1891, Conrad received from his guardian after returning from the Congo, and while physically disabled and seriously depressed: "I am sure that with your melancholy temperament you ought to avoid all meditations which lead to pessimistic conclusions. I advise you to lead a more active life than ever and to cultivate cheerful habits." Uneven in language on certain pages, and lacking "The Secret Sharer"'s economy, *Heart of Darkness* nevertheless remains one of the great dark meditations in literature, and one of the purest expressions of a melancholy temperament.

Heart of Darkness:
The Failure of Imagination

James Guetti

Heart of Darkness is apparently an account of one man's moral and psychological degeneration and of another's spatial and intellectual journey to understand the essentials of the matter. A reader expects that such a story will follow certain rules: the journey will be difficult, but at its end will be a meaningful disclosure in which the "degeneration" will be placed in a moral framework. I shall try to show in this discussion, however, that *Heart of Darkness* may be seen to deny, particularly, the relevance of such a moral framework and to question, generally, the possibilities of meaning for the journey itself—that as the narrative develops it is redefined so as to deny the basic assumptions upon which it appears to be constructed.

One of the two possible assertions of the title is this: the "darkness" has a "heart"; a reader penetrates the unknown and the partially known to the known. Marlow suggests throughout the story that at the center of things there is meaning and that he is pursuing this meaning. And yet the intensity of Marlow's inquiries serves only to emphasize the inconclusiveness of his findings. Again and again he seems about to declare the truth about Kurtz and the darkness, but his utterances most often take form in either a thunderous contradiction in terms or a hushed and introspective bemusement. In this manner we are left with the second and possibly the dominant assertion of the title in particular and *Heart of Darkness* in general: it is the

---

From *The Limits of Metaphor*. Cornell University Press, 1967. This essay originally appeared in *The Sewanee Review* 73, no. 3 (Summer 1965). © 1965 by the University of the South.

"heart," above all, that is composed of "darkness," there that the real darkness lies, and our progress must be through the apparently or partially known to the unknown.

The paradox implied in the title is nowhere more obvious than at what is usually taken to be the center of the story: Kurtz's death-bed cry, "The horror! The horror!" These words seem a response to the most private nightmare, to the unknown itself, but Marlow insists that they are quite the reverse: a "moment of complete knowledge." He asserts that "the horror" has to do not only with Kurtz's unspeakable history, but also with the world at large, "wide enough to embrace the whole universe, piercing enough to penetrate all the hearts that beat in the darkness." In attempting to resolve this apparent contradiction, we may inquire into what can be known of Kurtz's history.

Once he was an idealist of a kind, a member of the "new gang of virtue" of the trading company, and, according to Marlow, a man who apparently "had come out equipped with moral ideas of some sort." A complication of this view of Kurtz as a moral man is presented near the end of the story by a sometime journalist colleague: "'He electrified large meetings. He had faith—don't you see?—he had the faith.'" From the journalist's account to this point, a reader might be inclined to accept the possible but oversimple view of Kurtz as a clear case of moral degeneration; the man once possessed "the faith," which a reader may infer to be some high-minded and unambiguous creed, and then, in Africa, lost "the faith." Kurtz would have fallen, in these terms, within the framework of a traditional moral scheme, from a "heaven" to a "hell." But as the journalist continues, his description turns upon itself: "'the faith. He could get himself to believe anything—anything. He would have been a splendid leader of an extreme party.' 'What party?' I asked. 'Any party,' answered the other. 'He was an—an—extremist.' Did I not think so? I assented." Kurtz is characterized as a man who possessed all faiths, or any faith. Marlow, like a reader, momentarily does not understand this and asks, "What party?"—implying that he too conceives "the faith" as a single moral ideal to which Kurtz dedicated himself. But then the matter becomes clearer; "the faith" is some quality or ability that enabled Kurtz to believe in any creed whatsoever. With this assessment Marlow agrees.

The problem of the connection between Kurtz's eloquent and unscrupulous moral facility and Kurtz himself—his essential being—concerns Marlow more than any other. On the last stage of the voyage up the river to the Inner Station, with the blood of his "second-rate helmsman" in his shoes, he reflects this concern in a feeling of disappointment, as though the man he is seeking were "something altogether without a substance." Marlow imagines Kurtz not "as doing, you know, but as discoursing"; it is Kurtz's voice alone that is the man's "real presence," "his ability to talk, his words." Even after the actual, physical shock of Kurtz's appearance and, finally, of his death, Marlow insists, "The voice was gone. What else had been there? But I am of course aware that next day the pilgrims buried something in a muddy hole." The pilgrims buried an anonymous "something," as if Kurtz's reality were completely detached from Kurtz as defined by his voice.

The separation between Kurtz's speech and Kurtz's unvoiced self is often described in relation to his "degeneration." As Marlow contemplates the human heads upon posts near Kurtz's station, he remarks that "they only showed that Mr. Kurtz lacked restraint in the gratification of his various lusts, that there was something wanting in him—some small matter which, when the pressing need arose, could not be found under his magnificent eloquence." The "whisper" of the wilderness "echoed loudly within him because he was hollow at the core." It is thus suggested that Kurtz found himself in a world which—in comparison to civilization with its externally imposed restraints of law, social morality, and public opinion—was a world of enticing and dangerous possibilities, where a man must depend upon his "own innate strength," his "power of devotion . . . to an obscure backbreaking business." Kurtz had no such devotion; his capacity for arbitrary eloquence and belief left him "hollow at the core." "The faith," we may now suppose, was Kurtz's faith in himself, not as a moral being but as a being who could use or discard morality: Kurtz lived as if what was most essential about him were wholly separate from what he professed to believe. But this, Marlow insists, is not simply hypocrisy: "I had to deal with a being to whom I could not appeal in the name of anything high or low. I had, even like the niggers, to invoke him—himself—his own exalted and incredible degradation. There was nothing either above or below him, and I knew it. He had kicked himself loose of the earth. Confound the man! he had kicked the very earth to pieces." Kurtz's "degradation" is not the traditional result of a moral failure; it is "exalted and incredible," perhaps godlike; it is the effect of his setting himself apart fr⸺ the earth and the morality of the earth—apart, even, from the language of the earth with which he had such magnificent facility.

What Kurtz has done has general consequences. He has detached himself from the moral world, but in doing so he has, at least for Marlow, destroyed that world. Not simply has he "kicked himself loose of the earth," but "kicked the very earth to pieces." Kurtz's personal amorality has public ramifications, and Marlow is shaken; he declares—looking ahead to Kurtz's "the horror!"—that "no eloquence could have been so withering to one's belief in mankind as his final burst of sincerity." "Belief in mankind," I think, implies the moral nature of mankind, the very business in which Kurtz could be so adept, and in releasing himself from this moral nature, Kurtz has illustrated not only the possibility of such a release but also, as Marlow suggests, the possible inadequacy and irrelevance of morality to all men. Kurtz's "failure" thus becomes his achievement, and if that achievement remains partially a failure, the adequacy of moral codes is nonetheless questioned.

This problem is a familiar one to readers of Conrad. The imaginative, moral man enters a world of danger and enticement; he struggles, alone, to retain his morality. Often he fails. But in *Heart of Darkness* the matter is more complicated, for here the possible moralities, the means of restraint, may be seen to be less available—as alternatives, unreal. I have attempted to show something of the manner in which morality may be seen to fail Kurtz in *Heart of Darkness;* what follows is an account of the failure of morality in more pervasive terms.

Throughout the story a reader is confronted with various kinds of "restraint" that are clearly unsatisfactory. The chief accountant "accomplishes something" with his fastidious dress, for example, and the manager masks his envious and continual deceit with a hypocritical concern for saying and doing "the right thing." The most obvious case of this false kind of discipline is Marlow's native helmsman; he "thought all the world of himself. He was the most unstable kind of fool I had ever seen. He steered with no end of a swagger while you were by; but if he lost sight of you, he became instantly the prey of an abject funk, and would let that cripple of a steamboat get the upper hand of him in a minute."

In addition to these pseudomoralities, there are men for whom restraint is unnecessary: "you may be too much of a fool to go wrong—too dull even to know you are being assaulted by the powers of darkness. . . . Or you may be such a thunderingly exalted creature as to be altogether deaf and blind to anything but heavenly sights and sounds." None of these responses to the wilderness is possible for Marlow, nor, to Marlow's mind, for Kurtz. Both are men to whom the simpler falsehoods as morality do not appeal, and each, of course, possesses sufficient imagination to render him dangerously vulnerable to the "darkness."

Marlow declares that in confronting the wilderness, the "truth" of it, a man must "meet that truth with his own true stuff—with his own inborn strength. Principles won't do. Acquisitions, clothes, pretty rags—rags that would fly off at the first good shake. No; you want a deliberate belief." At this point Marlow's conception of restraint sounds fine indeed. He continues, asserting that when the wilderness appealed to him—as it must to every man—he had a "voice" of his own. Immediately following his testimonial to his own "voice," however, he admits that what prevented him from going "ashore for a howl and a dance" was only that he was too busy keeping his steamboat in one piece: "I had to mess about with whitelead . . . watch the steering, and circumvent those snags. . . . There was surface-truth enough in these things to save a wiser man." Marlow's ideal, as the kind of "truth" that a man may use to defend himself against the "truth" of the wilderness, is only a practical concern; it is founded upon keeping oneself busy, upon attending to matters of the surface.

Marlow says at one moment that it is in "work" that a man may "find" himself, his own "reality"; later, however, he appears to contradict himself and remarks, "When you have to attend to things of that sort, to the mere incidents of the surface, the reality—the reality, I tell you—fades. The inner truth is hidden—luckily, luckily. But I felt it all the same." As these quotations indicate, Marlow uses the term "reality" in two ways: the primary reality is the suggested essence of the wilderness, the darkness that must remain hidden if a man is to survive morally, while the secondary reality is a figurative reality like work, an artificial reality by which the truly real is concealed or even replaced. And Marlow admits that this reality of the second sort is simply a deluding activity, a fictitious play over the surface of things.

Marlow's account of his own restraint as a fiction reflects his nature as a "wanderer"; he is as morally rootless, perhaps, as Kurtz himself. In speaking of the "droll thing life is," Marlow describes his difficulties in a way that is suggestive in terms of Kurtz's experience:

> I have wrestled with death. It is the most unexciting contest you can imagine. It takes place in an impalpable grayness, with nothing underfoot, with nothing around, without spectators, without clamour, without glory, without the great desire of victory, without the great fear of defeat, in a sickly atmosphere of tepid skepticism, without much belief in your own right, and still less in that of your adversary. If such is the form of ultimate wisdom, then life is a greater riddle than some of us think it to be.

Marlow suggests that at certain moments—in struggling with death or, perhaps, with a wilderness—it is most difficult for a man to see any reality in a connection between moral "rights" and his experience; a man's most severe challenges are necessarily encountered in an "atmosphere of tepid skepticism." When Marlow himself struggles to keep the steamer afloat, struggles for his life, he replaces his own "tepid skepticism" with work; he is forced to do so by his physical danger. Kurtz's situation has by no means been so simple. Like Marlow, he had no dominating or saving "idea," but neither did he have Marlow's physical danger with its consequent activity—the work that luckily hides the reality.

In this manner Kurtz appears even more vulnerable than Marlow. For him the "tepid skepticism" was more intense; he viewed the disparity between his moral fictions and an amoral reality more starkly. Why he necessarily did so, I have considered only in part, but if we are to rely at all upon Marlow's insistence that Kurtz's experience corresponds to his own, then we may conclude for the moment that Kurtz's act of "kicking himself loose of the earth" was caused by his inability to save himself with fictions; when Kurtz's vision—the vision which Marlow assumes to be so similar to his own—destroyed the truth of morality and restraint, it also destroyed their availability.

It is on this account, I think, that Marlow refuses to condemn Kurtz in a moral way. The manager of the company remarks that Kurtz's "method" is "unsound," but Marlow denies this, asserting that it is "no method at all." The manager conceives that Kurtz *was* once a "remarkable man" when his method was sound, perhaps, but that since then he has gone wrong. Talk of "sound" or "unsound" is irrelevant for Marlow, however, and Kurtz *is* a "remarkable man" exactly because he has escaped the world of sound and unsound, because he has shown that such terms are inadequate as a measure of his experience. Kurtz's crime or achievement, then, is not that he has managed things badly for the company or, more generally, that he has sinned in a uniquely horrifying way, but that by means of an act of vision he has cut himself off from the possibility of sin. At the moment of this conversation with the manager, Marlow formally declares his sympathy with Kurtz.

Throughout *Heart of Darkness,* again, it is not simply the codes of the minor characters that are shown to be ignoble, nor is it only Marlow's code that is proved a tenuous fiction. Discipline in general is defined in the story not only as restraint, but also as a singleness of idea or intention—in contrast, of course, to something like Kurtz's multiple "faith" or to the infinite possibilities of the wilderness. This kind of spiritual rigidity is the important quality of the book which Marlow finds on his way to the Inner Station—*"An Inquiry into some Points of Seamanship"*: "Not a very enthralling book; but at the first glance you could see there a singleness of intention, an honest concern for the right way of going to work. . . . The simple old sailor, with his talk of chains and purchases, made me forget the jungle and the pilgrims in a delicious sensation of having come upon something unmistakably real." The "reality" of the book, its single-minded concern with work, is clearly the artificial or secondary reality that I have remarked, but it is more interesting to note here that when such reality seems possible, it seems so only in terms that are anomalous in the wilderness. It is apparent that this book is totally out of place in the jungle, that despite Marlow's desperate grasp on the book as a symbol of moral reality, this reality is rendered false and unreal by means of the very quality by which he declares it established: its irrelevance to the wilderness surrounding it.

In a similar manner, the wilderness may be seen elsewhere to deny singleness of purpose or, its equivalents, restraint and morality. As Marlow proceeds down the coast at the beginning of his journey, he encounters a French gunboat firing into the jungle:

> There wasn't even a shed there, and she was shelling the bush. It appears the French had one of their wars going on thereabouts. Her ensign dropped limp like a rag; the muz-

zles of the long six-inch guns stuck out all over the low
hull; the greasy, slimy swell swung her up lazily and let
her down, swaying her thin masts. In the empty immensity of earth, sky, and water, there she was, incomprehensible, firing into a continent. Pop, would go one of the six-
inch guns; a small flame would dart and vanish, a little
white smoke would disappear, a tiny projectile would give
a feeble screech—and nothing happened. Nothing could
happen.

War, with its polarities of life and death, victory and defeat, enemy
and enemy, may be seen generally as a straightforward matter. Guns,
too, are traditionally and rigidly purposeful, and when they are fired
something ought to happen. Here nothing happens: the guns "pop";
the projectiles are "feeble"; there is no enemy and no result. In a
parallel description, explosives are used at the first station to remove
a cliff: "The cliff was not in the way or anything; but this objectless
blasting was all the work going on." The blasting is not only "objectless," but also without effect, for "no change appeared on the face
of the rock." A moment later Marlow sees six natives—"crimi-
nals"—in chains, hears another explosion, and then synthesizes these
phenomena with his recollection of the gunboat:

> Another report from the cliff made me think suddenly of
> that ship of war I had seen firing into a continent. It was
> the same kind of ominous voice; but these men could by
> no stretch of imagination be called enemies. They were
> called criminals, and the outraged law, like the burst-
> ing shells, had come to them, an insoluble mystery from
> the sea.

The law—with its apparent, straightforward purpose—like the
shells and the blasting has been negated; it has become a mystery,
incomprehensible, and has no effect as law, but merely renders the
savages indifferent and unhappy. Here the law, the blasting, and the
warfare, then, are characterized as having no disciplined purpose or
effect, and the disparity between these devices of civilization and the
wilderness which they attempt corresponds to the disparity between
morality and the wilderness mentioned previously. The scope of this
disparity between human schemes and the wilderness, as we proceed
through the story, is ever widening.

It has been remarked here that Marlow's own capacity for re-straint in Africa depends upon his busy thoughtlessness, and he has said that this restraint reflects a concern only with the incidents of the surface, as opposed to the "reality" at the heart. The narrator who begins *Heart of Darkness* defines Marlow's manner of storytell-ing in a way that is puzzling yet clearly analogous to Marlow's own characterizations of his moral attitude:

> The yarns of seamen have a direct simplicity, the whole meaning of which lies within the shell of a cracked nut. But Marlow was not typical . . . and to him the meaning of an episode was not inside like a kernel but outside, en-veloping the tale which brought it out only as a glow brings out a haze, in the likeness of one of these misty halos that sometimes are made visible by the spectral illu-mination of moonshine.

In *Heart of Darkness* we observe Marlow moving along the coast of the wilderness or over the surface of the river, and here we encounter the idea of his language moving over the outside of an "episode," surrounding the episode but never penetrating it. Marlow's attempts at meaning in general, then, take the same form as his attempts at morality in particular. Both meaning and morality are seen to be matters of the surface or exterior, while the reality—not Marlow's artificial reality but the reality beyond surfaces—is something deep within, something at the center that is not approached. There is an important difference, however, between Marlow's moral attitudes and his more generally meaningful attitudes: in the first instance he continually suggests that it would be imprudent to look beneath the surface; in the second he just as frequently admits that it is impossible to do so.

The emphasis of the passage quoted above is affirmative; the narrator implies that the search for meaning can be satisfied, some-how, in a concern with the exterior. And yet the very structure of *Heart of Darkness*—with the journey to the Inner Station, toward the man who constitutes the end of the search, and, certainly, toward some meaning in terms of the pervasive metaphor of "meaning at the heart"—seems to assert that there is a more significant reality within; the fact of the search for Kurtz and for some disclosure con-cerning him implies that matters of the surface are not enough.

Previously I have suggested that Kurtz remains a voice for Marlow, even after Marlow has confronted him at the Inner Station, and that upon Kurtz's death Marlow exhibits his uncertainty as to whether there was ever anything else to the man but a voice, admitting only that the pilgrims buried "something." This attitude toward Kurtz—and it is never modified—implies a failure by Marlow, for although he struggles into the heart of darkness, declares his sympathetic allegiance to Kurtz, watches the man die, and journeys out again, he ends where he began. Marlow remarks the futility of his position more than once: "arguing with myself whether or no I would talk openly with Kurtz; but before I could come to any conclusion it occurred to me that my speech or my silence, indeed any action of mine, would be a mere futility. . . . The essentials of this affair lay deep under the surface, beyond my reach, and beyond my power of meddling."

Marlow's conception of the reality of the wilderness remains as bemused as his idea of the meaning of Kurtz's experience. Although he constantly suggests that at the center of the wilderness lies "the amazing reality of its concealed life," and although he often asserts that he is penetrating "deeper and deeper into the heart of darkness," in his insistence upon the vague and the paradoxical the "purpose" of the wilderness remains always "inscrutable." It escapes definition except in terms of its awesome, vague, and passive magnitude: "the silent wilderness surrounding this cleared speck on the earth struck me as something great and invincible, like evil or truth." Marlow is no nearer a central reality at the geographical heart of the darkness than he was when, proceeding down the coast, he was aware of a "general sense of vague and oppressive wonder."

It thus seems generally impossible to move beyond the surface in any meaningful way. Reality in this story exists not in the positive but in the negative, for it is all that human disciplines cannot reach, all that lies beyond these disciplines within the center of a man, of a wilderness, and, as Marlow implies, of experience itself. Language too, as all resources of the human imagination, fails in attempting to discover the meaning of Kurtz and of experience: "He was just a word for me. I did not see the man in the name any more than you do. Do you see him? Do you see the story? Do you see anything? . . . No, it is impossible; it is impossible to convey the life-sensation of any given epoch of one's existence—that which makes its truth, its meaning—its subtle and penetrating essence. It is impossible. We live, as we dream—alone." Kurtz was a word and remained a word, even when he and Marlow were face to face: attempts to discover a meaning beyond the word failed. And Marlow is not speaking only of Kurtz. He begins with his inability to convey some meaning in terms of Kurtz in Africa, but he continues, characteristically, with the insistence that this inability is universal, that by focusing on Kurtz's particular "aloneness" or remoteness from the world of language there is revealed a general condition of human experience.

Language has meaning, in *Heart of Darkness,* in relation to the exteriors of experience—the coast of a wilderness, the surface of a river, a man's appearance and his voice—and this meaning can exist as a reality so long as one remains ignorant, deliberately or otherwise, of all that lies beyond these exteriors, of what language cannot penetrate. For with the intimation that there is something beyond the verbal and, indeed, the imaginative capacities comes the realization that language is insufficient. And if we desire to discover a reality greater than that of words, we are confronted not with the truth within, but with the real disparity between the gimmickry of the human mind and this truth. Because Marlow wishes to know more than surfaces, the reality of surfaces is destroyed. His knowledge of reality may now exist only as his knowledge of the unbridgeable separation between the world of man's disciplined imagination and that something or nothing to which this world is assumed to relate.

Thus whereas Marlow uses the term "reality" in two ways, the reality that he—and a reader—discovers is of a third sort. It is a reality that exists in the realization that "surface" and "heart" are inevitably separate matters and that mind can have ordered awareness only of the former. Marlow's final reality is a state of suspension between the disciplined world of mind and language and the world of essences at the center of experience—whatever these may be—which mind attempts to apprehend but cannot, a dream-state of suggestions and futilities. Marlow is finally aware of both sorts of "reality," certain of neither.

It is for these reasons that Marlow does not view Kurtz's last utterance only as a cry of selfish despair, but declares that Kurtz had "summed up." And as a summation of the imaginative experience of *Heart of Darkness,* "the horror!" can have but one meaning: all hearts are in darkness; the morality and meaning with which man surrounds himself and his experience is unreal; the reality of experience lies beyond language and the processes of the human imagination. In revealing this knowledge to Marlow, Kurtz has taken a step that

Marlow would not take explicitly: "he had made that last stride, he had stepped over the edge, while I had been permitted to draw back my hesitating foot." Because he has relinquished his hold upon his ideals and his eloquence, because he has wholly detached himself from matters of the surface, Kurtz is able at last to define, as Marlow sees it, that about which Marlow himself—in his preoccupation with both the reality of the surface and the reality of the "heart"—has been so reluctant and so ambiguous. Marlow is torn, throughout the story, between the desire to achieve a realization as final as Kurtz's and the conviction that he must deny such a realization if his life is to have any meaning. Kurtz is destroyed in his movement toward and final confrontation of what Marlow views as the ultimate truth: that the essentials of experience remain amoral and, even, alinguistic.

Heart of Darkness, then, as the account of a journey into the center of things—of Africa, of Kurtz, of Marlow, and of human existence—poses itself as the refutation of such a journey and as the refutation of the general metaphorical conception that meaning may be found within, beneath, at the center. At the end of the search we encounter a darkness, and it is no more defined than at the beginning of the journey and the narrative; it continues to exist only as something unapproachable. The stages of such a journey and such a discourse, the struggle with vagueness and paradox, accompanied always with the feeling that one is not yet at the heart of the matter, must suffice. Once again amid the disciplines and meanings of civilization that are so easily and carelessly assumed to be real, Marlow calls to mind his experience beyond these meanings and declares that anxious ministrations to his weakened body are beside the point: "it was my imagination that wanted soothing."

*H*eart of Darkness:
A Choice of Nightmares?

C. B. Cox

> *He that can with* Epicurus *content his Ideas with the* Films *and* Images *that fly off upon his Senses from the* Superficies *of Things; Such a Man truly wise, creams off Nature, leaving the Sower and the Dregs, for Philosophy and Reason to lap up. This is the sublime and refined Point of Felicity, called,* The Possession of being well deceived; *The Serene Peaceful State of being a Fool among Knaves.*
>
> —SWIFT, *A Tale of a Tub*

Kurtz's native woman appears to Marlow as a wild and gorgeous apparition. She is savage and superb, he tells us, wild-eyed and magnificent. She treads the earth proudly, her body covered with barbarous ornaments, her hair arranged in the shape of a helmet. For Marlow she embodies the spirit of the dark forests: "And in the hush that had fallen suddenly upon the whole sorrowful land, the immense wilderness, the colossal body of the fecund and mysterious life seemed to look at her, pensive, as though it had been looking at the image of its own tenebrous and passionate soul." She regards the pilgrims on Marlow's steamer without a stir, "like the wilderness itself, with an air of brooding over an inscrutable purpose."

If we compare this splendid savage with Kurtz's European fiancée, his Intended, it may seem that we are setting side by side dynamic energy with sterile hypocrisy, life with death. The savage is tragic and fierce; we may take it for granted that Kurtz has enjoyed

---

From *Joseph Conrad: The Modern Imagination.* © 1974 by C. B. Cox. Rowman & Littlefield, 1974.

sexual orgies with her in his role as a worshipped god to whom
human sacrifices are offered. Her Dionysiac passions might seem
more attractive in their vitality than the living tomb the Intended has
created for herself in Brussels. As often in Conrad, objects associated
with human beings take on appropriate characteristics. The Intended
lives in a house in a street as still and decorous as a well-kept alley in
a cemetery. Her tall marble fireplace has a cold and monumental
whiteness, and her grand piano gleams like a sombre and polished
sarcophagus. She has chosen for herself a graveyard, where she can
exist in comfort only through a lie; her condition symbolizes that of
Western Europe. In contrast, the savage lives out her sexual urges as
naturally as if she were a wild beast.

Yet there is something detestable, even loathsome, about this
primitive creature. The youthful Russian, whom Kurtz befriends in
the forests, tells Marlow how she wanted him killed for taking rags
from the storeroom to mend his clothes. The unspeakable rites in
which she has participated presumably include torture and killings.
Cohabitation with this superb but mindless creature degrades Kurtz;
for Conrad's total response to her, as to the wilderness, mixes together the attractive and the repellent.

The novel can be interpreted in a Freudian manner as a journey
into the wilderness of sex, a fantasy shaped by Conrad's own divided
impulses. The pilgrims penetrate down a narrow channel to find, in
the darkness, a violent orgiastic experience. Kurtz, the outlaw-
figure, has dared to transgress the restraints imposed by civilization.
He represents Marlow's shadow self, the secret sharer, and the voyage of exploration is a night journey into the unconscious, or a discovery of the Freudian id. From this point of view, the imprecision
of Conrad's language in descriptions of the wilderness could be a
subconscious evasion of the truth, a fascinated hovering around a
subject whose realities he dare not fully acknowledge. Elsewhere, as
Bernard Meyer has shown, Conrad's reaction to sex seems maso-
chistic and fearful. The helmet-like hair is characteristic of other
Conrad heroines, notably Felicia Moorsom in "The Planter of Mal-
ata," whose lover enjoys self-abasement before her power. Should we
interpret the whole fearful journey, therefore, as a sign of Conrad's
repressed nightmares, his desire for a sexual initiation whose demands might prove him impotent?

When such Freudian interpretations are put forward as complete
explanations, they become reductive. Conrad's impressionist

method gathers into itself a wealth of possible meanings of which the Freudian constitute only a part. Nor do I agree with E. M. Forster or F. R. Leavis, who find the treatment of the wilderness too imprecise. The darkness exists as a literary symbol, whose paraphrasable meanings can never do full justice to the richness of this poetic meditation on human existence. The novel contrasts the savage woman with the Intended, Western civilization with primitive Africa, the language of the rational mind, of concrete imagery and recognizable forms, with a mystery at the heart of consciousness beyond expression in words. Like Marlow, we are offered a choice of nightmares, but the strategy of the novel suggests that final commitment is possible only for the simple and the deluded. The story is a powerful fable of the divided consciousness, of the warring values of passion and restraint.

II

Conrad's own experience of the Congo covered only six months, from June to December 1890. From his notebook and letters we can glimpse why the adventure was so traumatic. At Matadi, about forty miles up the river, he watched the Africans organized into chain gangs, driven to the point of exhaustion. He records with horror his disgust for the Belgians' vile scramble for loot. On July 3, 1890, he writes in his notebook: "Saw at a camp place the dead body of a Backongo. Shot? Horrid smell." He was quickly shipped out of the country with the fever and malarial gout which remained with him for the rest of his life.

Like Conrad, Marlow enrols as a servant of a Trading Company in Brussels, the "city that always makes me think of a whited sepulchre." In the office he is received by the enigmatic ladies, knitting black wool, who guard the door of Darkness. They are like the Fates, Clotho and Atropos, spinning and breaking the thread of each man's life. In many respects Marlow's journey down the Congo parallels the classic expedition to the underworld, passing through the circles of Hell, the Company Station, the Central Station and the Inner Station, where he meets Kurtz, the devil incarnate.

But such correspondences should not be pushed too far. Conrad's intention is to surround his story with an aura of poetic allusion, rather than to compose an explicit allegory. On a first reading Marlow's journey towards "the centre of the earth" grips our attention like a conventional thriller; the setting is exotic, and we are carried forward through moments of danger, escapes, unexpected attack. But even on a first reading we are disturbed by a pervasive irony. The journey appears to be a kind of parody of the romantic quest for the Grail. Marlow ironically calls his debased, greedy companions "pilgrims," and the manager even builds an Arthurian round table to prevent his subordinates from quarrelling about precedence. Marlow seems to be the one true pilgrim, determined to make contact with the reality of Kurtz. The quest comes to represent for him retrospectively the culminating point of his experience: "It seemed somehow to throw a kind of light on everything about me—and into my thought." He embarks on an intellectual journey into the secret meanings of consciousness. But, as always, Marlow's narration is tortuous and ambiguous, and we are not sure whether he finds the Grail. The anonymous narrator informs us, as the story is told to a group of friends on the cruising yawl on the Thames, that we are about to hear "one of Marlow's inconclusive experiences."

James Guetti's *The Limits of Metaphor* includes a brilliant analysis of *Heart of Darkness*. He points out that the title itself can be interpreted in two different ways. Heart of darkness may suggest that the wilderness has a heart, which the reader, guided by Marlow, may discover. At the centre of existence we may find the secret meaning of the pilgrimage. But heart of darkness may also imply that the real darkness is in the heart, and that we journey from the known to the unknown. We are led towards an ultimate darkness, a condition of meaninglessness, which negates all civilized values.

Marlow's uncertainties are seen in his contradictory use of the word "reality." When trying to repair the battered, tin-pot steamboat, for example, he tells us:

> I don't like work—no man does—but I like what is in the work,—the chance to find yourself. Your own reality—for yourself, not for others—what no other man can ever know. They can only see the mere show, and never can tell what it really means.

Only a few pages later he describes how the wilderness, "the overwhelming realities of this strange world of plants, and water, and silences," regarded the pilgrims with a vengeful aspect. His own absorption in the work of keeping the steamboat afloat helped him to avoid the frightening stillness of the forest:

> When you have to attend to things of that sort, to the mere
> incidents of the surface, the reality—the reality, I tell
> you—fades. The inner truth is hidden—luckily, luckily.
> But I felt it all the same; I felt often its mysterious stillness
> watching me at my monkey tricks, just as it watches you
> fellows performing on your respective tight-ropes for—
> what is it? half-a-crown a tumble—.

Is work "monkey tricks" or self-discovery? Is the wilderness the primary reality, and Marlow's occupation on the steamboat merely an
artificial fiction which conceals the truth from him? The novel oscil-
lates, wanders, between these two definitions of "reality."

As in *Lord Jim,* the quest is both a search for moral enlighten-
ment and an investigation into the appropriateness of aesthetic
forms. As he turns his gaze away from the brooding stillness of the
forests, Marlow knows that Kurtz has dared to commit himself to a
barbarism both seductive and dangerous: it may be imprudent to
look below the surface. At the same time, Marlow understands that
it is probably impossible to find a suitable language to describe the
wilderness; words are part of the world of surfaces. "What was in
there?" Marlow asks himself quite early in his adventures: "somehow
it didn't bring any image with it—no more than if I had been told an
angel or a fiend was in there." As he journeys down the coast of
Africa on his way to the Congo, he notes that the landscape is "featureless"; his artistic problem is that the wilderness impresses him as
a kind of disembodied presence.

In *The Great Tradition,* F. R. Leavis takes for granted that symbols work only when anchored to a record of immediate sensations,
when they totally coincide with the concrete presentment of incident, setting and image. Because of this assumption, he condemns
the imprecision of parts of *Heart of Darkness,* and draws attention to
the intrusion of words such as "incomprehensible," "inscrutable," or
"mysterious"; whose "actual effect is not to magnify but rather to
muffle":

> He [Conrad] is intent on making a virtue out of not know-
> ing what he means. The vague and unrealizable, he asserts
> with a strained impressiveness, is the profoundly and tre-
> mendously significant.

But, as I argued [elsewhere], Conrad is deliberately creating a kind
of writing which draws attention to its own inadequacies. He is seek-

ing for an artistic form to capture an awareness beyond the area of immediate sensation. This language must in some ways remain "featureless," because no images taken directly from the senses will suffice. The temptation for the artist, as Conrad sees it, would be to offer his readers an organizing metaphor by which they could comprehend both his values and his aesthetic forms, a heart for his awareness of darkness. It is a tribute to his courage, both as man and artist, that in this story he resists the seduction of the ultimate symbol. Marlow acknowledges that he can only achieve ordered awareness of the surfaces of life, and that the essence, the wilderness, must escape his definitions. He repeatedly uses the words "as if" to suggest that his similes carry only a provisional status. The "as if" construction gives Conrad the freedom to shape experience in terms of human language, and yet still to imply doubt about its final validity.

This insistence on the failure of civilized language is a central purpose of the novel, illustrated not only when Marlow despairingly admits that words cannot express his experience but also in the symbolism. On several occasions the representatives of Europe shoot into the wilderness. The French man-of-war shells the bush, incomprehensibly firing into a continent. Its tiny projectiles screech feebly, and nothing happens. The pilgrims let loose a volley at Kurtz's natives, and again their efforts seem absurd: "The pilgrims had opened with their Winchesters, and were simply squirting lead into that bush." Representative of Africa is the old hippo who roams at night over the station grounds. The pilgrims empty every rifle they can lay their hands on at him, but he bears a charmed life. This uselessness of European weapons parallels the failure of civilized discourse to make any impression on the wilderness. The mystery defies the usual conventions of storytelling.

Heart of Darkness includes a famous description of Marlow's indirect method of narration. The anonymous narrator on the yawl tells us:

> The yarns of seamen have a direct simplicity, the whole meaning of which lies within the shell of a cracked nut. But Marlow was not typical (if his propensity to spin yarns be excepted), and to him the meaning of an episode was not inside like a kernel but outside, enveloping the tale which brought it out only as a glow brings out a haze, in the likeness of one of these misty halos that sometimes are made visible by the spectral illumination of moonshine.

Marlow knows he cannot penetrate to the centre, to the heart. In this sense his journey to Kurtz can never end in a final, satisfying discovery; yet he can create "a glow," "a haze," so that his listeners may progress in some degree towards an apprehension of his experience. He deplores that "it is impossible to convey the life-sensation of any given epoch of one's existence—that which makes its truth, its meaning—its subtle and penetrating essence. It is impossible. We live, as we dream—alone." But his journey, and his decision to tell his tale, arouse a hope that we may achieve some insight, that the heart may not be entirely impenetrable. As he speaks to his companions on the cruising yawl, it is for the anonymous narrator like listening to the voice of darkness. He feels faintly uneasy, as the narrative shapes itself "without human lips in the heavy night-air of the river." Guetti defines Marlow's final reality as "a state of suspension between the disciplined world of mind and language and the world of essences at the centre of experience." Perhaps this "suspension" justifies the Buddha-like pose Marlow assumes while telling his story. Both forms of morality, both kinds of language, make their separate claims, and the man of vision must accept the burden of the double consciousness.

III

Peter Garrett makes a clear contrast between the two forms of narrative. At first the sordid farce of imperialism is presented in an imagistic manner, but as the narrative progresses the centre of attention shifts to the wilderness. Imperialist corruption is anatomized in sharp, visual images, and a clear moral viewpoint is presented, a scheme of values preserved by Marlow in his devotion to the work ethic. In contrast, the wilderness is evoked in portentous, rhetorical language which creates an indefinitely metaphysical meaningfulness, an inner "reality" which threatens all moral significance. The tale expresses an unresolved tension between the two.

Conrad's disgust at what he witnessed in the Congo, his savage contempt for the Belgian colonists, gives *Heart of Darkness* an important public dimension. Many writers on Conrad have assumed this social and economic commentary to be central to the story, and have considered Kurtz as the supreme example of European hypocrisy. This sense of outrage invests the scenes at Matadi with a symbolic status as horrifyingly representative of civilized lunacy. The European machines prove useless, like beasts dying in an alien environment. A boiler wallows purposelessly in the grass; an undersized railway truck lies on its back, like a dead carcass of some animal, with its wheels in the air. Dull detonations mark the attempt to blast away the rock for a railway, but the explosion is described as ridiculous and ineffective like some incident in Kafka. No change appears on the face of the rock: "The cliff was not in the way or anything; but this objectless blasting was all the work going on." The unhappy savages die off in the grove of death, like souls in the gloomy circle of some Inferno. Conrad's language is bitter and furious at this wanton smashup, this dehumanization of landscape and people.

The white human beings who greedily scramble for the ivory are all hollow men. The fastidious chief accountant is a hairdresser's dummy who has avoided the surrounding horror by merging his identity in his elegant clothes and the correct entries in his accounts. The brickmaker, who never makes bricks, is called "a papier-mâché Mephistopheles"; Marlow expects that if he poked his finger through him he would find nothing inside but a little loose dirt. We suspect that the manager is never ill because he has no innards upon which the germs could latch. After Marlow has overheard their conversation, the manager and his uncle depart "tugging painfully uphill their two ridiculous shadows of unequal length, that trailed behind them slowly over the tall grass without bending a single blade." These men are ghosts, whose fantastic invasion can effect no permanent change on the wilderness.

Conrad expresses profound compassion for the sick negroes, and later even for the starving cannibals. This should be remembered when he is accused of an absolute nihilism. This care for humanity, mediated through the thoughts of Marlow, is linked with the work-ethic. We admire Marlow because he feels such sympathies, and because he can manage the steamboat. While the pilgrims fire uselessly into the bush, he disperses the attacking natives by pulling the boat's whistle.

Such work is not just a keeping up of appearances, an evasion of the wilderness, but retains its own value. Like Marlow, we respect the cannibals, who "were men one could work with." The Russian's book, *An Inquiry into some Points of Seamanship,* strikes Marlow as "unmistakably real." The author's singleness of intention, "an honest concern for the right way of going to work," makes these pages "luminous": "I assure you to leave off reading was like tearing myself away from the shelter of an old and solid friendship." The prevailing irony makes this tattered manuscript in the heart of a wilderness seem also absurd and irrelevant. But the darkness cannot always extinguish these lights. The two sets of values, darkness and light, strive unsuccessfully for a complete mastery. As he contemplates the contemporary hell which is London, the growing darkness over the Thames from which the story emerges, Marlow prays that we may live on in the light created by real men: "We live in the flicker—may it last as long as the old earth keeps rolling!" Civilization, to which the anonymous narrator gives a more fulsome tribute, is not without its virtues, and involves the metamorphosis of darkness into light. As J. Hillis Miller points out in *Poets of Reality,* it is a process of transforming everything unknown, irrational or indistinct into clear forms, named and ordered, given a meaning and use by man. To be safe, we must have a blind devotion to immediate practical tasks, to the needs of this ordered world. Marlow's greatness is that he is not content just to be safe, and that, in contrast with the pilgrims, he craves speech with Kurtz. At the same time, his cult of efficiency, his successful caring for the people in his charge, is far from a despicable illusion.

IV

Conrad's description of the wilderness depends on incremental repetition, on the resonance of drawn-out brooding sentences, on interweavings of darkness and light. The reader must respond to the strange music of the rhythms, to a sense of great tracts of time and unknown mysteries. The fascination of the abomination, to which a decent Roman citizen might have responded in Britain centuries ago, is present in the wandering ritualistic style. Many writers on this story have missed this crucial element, and concentrated solely on the sense of moral outrage.

The first blacks seen by Marlow on his journey to the Congo possess a "wild vitality, an intense energy of movement, that was as natural and true as the surf along their coast." Like Kurtz's mistress, they exist in a natural relation with the land. They belong, Marlow thinks, to "a world of straight-forward facts," in contrast to the absurd endeavours of the Europeans to civilize the darkness. As he proceeds along the river, the drums speak to him with "a sound weird, appealing, suggestive, and wild—and perhaps with as profound a meaning as the sound of bells in a Christian country." He gradually assumes that the wilderness is alive, either making an appeal or offering a menace. Conrad tries to express the *force* of this silent presence:

> The great wall of vegetation, an exuberant and entangled mass of trunks, branches, leaves, boughs, festoons, motionless in the moonlight, was like a rioting invasion of soundless life, a rolling wave of plants, piled up, crested, ready to topple over the creek, to sweep every little man of us out of his little existence. And it moved not. A deadened burst of mighty splashes and snorts reached us from afar, as though an ichthyosaurus had been taking a bath of glitter in the great river.

Conrad is trying to suggest a menacing force which encircles all forms of civilization, a presence of universal destruction we acknowledge but cannot control or even properly understand. The creature in the river typifies this sort of mental image, for he is a denizen of another earth. He recalls for Marlow a memory of an ichthyosaurus; he is bathing not in water but in the glitter of the moonlight. The burst of splashes is deadened, muted, as if our apprehension of these realities must inevitably reach us from an inaccessible distance. In *Four Quartets,* T. S. Eliot describes a stillness "heard, half-heard, between two waves of the sea." The wilderness is similarly only partially apprehended. Marlow feels bewitched, "cut off for ever from everything you had known once—somewhere—far away—in another existence perhaps." They are "wanderers on prehistoric earth, on an earth that wore the aspect of an unknown planet." The stillness does not in the least resemble a peace: "It was the stillness of an implacable force brooding over an inscrutable intention." These sentences bring into our mind the smallness of our forms of apprehension, our distinctions and categories. The mystery breathes around us, stirring up strange fears, promising strange freedoms. The natives howl and leap in the wilderness, betraying to Marlow remote kinship with this wild and passionate uproar. By concentrating on his work he resists the temptation to go ashore for a howl or a dance. The wilderness is an immensity of natural chaos, just beyond the reach of consciousness. Marlow says: "The inner truth is hidden—luckily, luckily. But I felt it all the same."

The quest ends in white fog, warm and clammy, more blinding

than the night. The eyes of the pilgrims are of no more use to them than if they had been "buried miles deep in a heap of cotton-wool." This vivid, nightmare experience symbolizes the blotting out of all civilized distinctions, an entry into a non-mental world. These moments are the culmination of all Marlow's descriptions of the wilderness. Because of his sense of the insecurity of intelligence, Conrad invites his readers to participate vicariously in a condition devoid of sensation, a blacking out of perception in a trance where unknown realities may make their presence felt. When Marlow hears the loud cry of desolation of the savages, it is "as though the mist itself had screamed." This is a moment of revelation, an epiphany of the Savage God. In this all-embracing mist Europe's lights seem momentary flickers about to be snuffed out by a darkness both liberating and destructive.

V

Kurtz has responded to this vision. As an emissary of science and progress, he travelled to Africa to campaign for the ideal. He is a painter, writer, musician and political orator, apparently combining in himself the values of a high culture. But away from society he is liberated to do anything, either good or evil. He shakes himself free from restraints, and becomes his own diabolical God: "He had kicked himself loose of the earth . . . he had kicked the very earth to pieces. He was alone, and I before him did not know whether I stood on the ground or floated in the air." The wilderness has found him out, has whispered things to him about himself, has patted him on the head, turned him bald, "and, behold, it was like a ball—an ivory ball." With a perverse sense of humour, the darkness has metamorphosed Kurtz into the object for which he craves, the ivory, and has infiltrated itself into his blood and bones. What, then, is the value of his freedom? It is on this issue that all the critics disagree.

Writing in 1932, Joseph Warren Beach adopted a straightforward moral stance: "Kurtz is a personal embodiment, a dramatization of all that Conrad felt of futility, degradation and horror in what the Europeans in the Congo called 'progress,' which meant the exploitation of the natives by every variety of cruelty and treachery known to greedy man." A completely opposite view is taken by K. K. Ruthven, who thinks of Kurtz as a hero. In "The Savage God: Conrad and Lawrence," he draws attention to the way much twentieth-century art has been fascinated by the primitive. A destructive hatred of civilization, most obvious in D. H. Lawrence, seems in many ways vindicated by the findings of Frazerian anthropology and Freudian psychology. The new discoveries in both these areas defend the integrity of the prelogical, analogical or illogical qualities of consciousness: the whole man is said to thrive in a primitive environment. From this point of view, *Heart of Darkness* is an attack on the values of Western society, and an annunciation of the Savage God. The choice of nightmares is between a bad Europe and a bad Africa. But whereas Europe is a sepulchre, Africa is horrific and vital. Marlow, according to this theory, remains solidly Victorian in his adherence to the work ethic, while Conrad's heroes, such as Kurtz, immerse themselves in the destructive element. Kurtz releases his id from European restraint; he is a pioneer in a psychic wilderness. Ruthven believes Conrad was in sympathy with Kurtz, who as pioneer must die before his emancipation from European values is complete.

Lionel Trilling does not go to this extreme, but he too sees Kurtz as a hero of the spirit. He admits that for him it is still ambiguous whether Kurtz's famous deathbed cry "The horror! The horror!" refers to the approach of death, or to his experience of savage life:

> Whichever it is, to Marlow the fact that Kurtz could utter this cry at the point of death, while Marlow himself, when death threatens him, can know it only as a weary grayness, marks the difference between the ordinary man and a hero of the spirit. Is this not the essence of the modern belief about the nature of the artist, the man who goes down into that hell which is the historical beginning of the human soul, a beginning not outgrown but established in humanity as we know it now, preferring the reality of this hell to the bland lies of the civilization that has overlaid it?

Trilling compares *Heart of Darkness* to Thomas Mann's *Death in Venice,* in which Aschenbach's submission to his lust for a beautiful young boy, the conquest of his ethical reason by Dionysian eroticism, is taken by us not as a defeat but as a kind of terrible rebirth.

These views, particularly those of Ruthven, give insufficient emphasis to the moral condemnation of Kurtz. He has exploited the natives most shamefully. His megalomania as he lies dying strikes

Marlow as at times contemptibly childish. He dreams of kings meeting him at railway-stations on his return from some ghastly Nowhere, where he would have accomplished great things. He is avid of lying fame, of sham distinction, of all the appearances of success and power.

The wilderness whispers to Kurtz with an irresistible fascination because he is "hollow at the core." Does this mean that he is another hollow man, like the brickmaker and the manager? Clearly not, for these characters have not the courage to respond to the darkness. Their death-in-life condition makes them impervious to its attractions; unlike Marlow, they feel no temptation to set off for a howl or a dance. Like so many of Marlow's pronouncements, this use of "hollow" echoes ambiguously through the novel. Kurtz's identity reduces itself to a voice, to a display of rhetoric. This is true of his seventeen-page report to the International Society for the Suppression of Savage Customs, whose enthusiastic idealism we may treat with contempt. Its final scrawled note: "Exterminate all the brutes!" blows the rhetoric away like smoke in a sudden gust of wind.

But Kurtz's personal rhetoric seduces the innocent Russian by its strange charm, its revelation of infinite possibilities. Marlow himself is appalled by the strange effect of Kurtz's words: "They had behind them, to my mind, the terrific suggestiveness of words heard in dreams, of phrases spoken in nightmares." The rhetoric, like Kurtz, wanders in freedom, untrammelled by conventional moral or practical norms. He has achieved a diabolical, Faustian liberty, which rejects European ideas as limiting illusions. His rhetoric may lack the honesty to fact exemplified in the lucid prose of *An Inquiry into some Points of Seamanship*. He is indeed a natural extremist, who, as the journalist tells Marlow after his return to Europe, could have used his eloquence for any cause. But at crucial moments, as when he confronts death itself, his vision comprehends the disparity between the lies of civilization and the primal realities of Africa.

When Kurtz drags himself from the steamboat, and crawls on all fours down the trail towards the savages, Marlow acts with great courage by pursuing him into the wilderness. He acknowledges that he might succumb to its temptations, and he dreams of living alone and unarmed in the forests to an advanced age. But it is his duty to bring the devil back to the security of the steamboat, to make the shadow submit to the orderly world of civilization. His success ends with the death of Kurtz, and we sense that Marlow, at least temporarily, has overcome the dragon in the abyss of his own consciousness.

The most fantastic creature in the forests is the Russian, who because of his patchwork clothes resembles a harlequin. His face is like the autumn sky, overcast one moment and bright the next. His naïve enthusiasm for Kurtz is another element in the riddle. "This man has enlarged my mind," he tells Marlow. Are we entitled to sneer? His existence is fabulous, and Marlow expects him instantly to disappear. To the harlequin, Kurtz has discoursed on everything, even love, and the rhetoric—so false?—has aroused in the Russian a fanatical loyalty. He retains a purity, a selflessness which Marlow envies: "He surely wanted nothing from the wilderness but space to breathe in and to push on through." The harlequin introduces a further dimension. Kurtz is degraded, exalted, tragic; Brussels is civilized, hypocritical, dead. The harlequin represents the pure spirit of youth, still free from the corruption of both sets of values.

The strain breaks Marlow, and illness takes him to the borders of death. After his recovery, his experience at first makes it impossible for him to reconcile himself to the workaday world of Brussels. Like Gulliver, he feels contempt for the inferior humans who hurry through the streets with their insignificant and silly dreams. He himself is haunted by a different kind of dream, by an awareness which makes Brussels, the sepulchral city, a place of folly and pretence. What is the nature of this dream? Marlow admits that the essentials lie deep under the surface, beyond his reach and beyond his power of meddling. He is trying to tell us a dream, and therefore "making a vain attempt, because no relation of a dream can convey the dream-sensation, that commingling of absurdity, surprise and bewilderment in a tremor of struggling revolt, that notion of being captured by the incredible which is of the very essence of dreams." He remains suspended between two irreconcilable worlds.

And so the narrative circles back to its beginnings, for no awakening from the nightmare is possible. Marlow is back on the Thames, telling his story, surrounded by memories of times when Britain herself was lost in savagery, and thinking that civilization is a continual, unsuccessful journey to conquer a wilderness. The last episode of his adventure, when he returns some relics of Kurtz to his Intended, gathers into itself all the ambiguities concerning the heart of darkness.

VI

F. R. Leavis dislikes this final scene with the Intended. The irony, in his view, lies in the contrast between her innocent nobility, her purity of idealizing faith, and the corruption of Kurtz. "Nobility" seems to me the wrong word to use for the Intended, and I do not agree that there is nothing ironical in the presentment of her. We have already seen how her home is a graveyard. It is appropriate that Marlow should lie to her, should tell her Kurtz's last words were her name, for her life is based on hypocrisy, like the European civilization in which she has been nurtured. Her devotion has transformed the reality of Kurtz into a false ideal, and this self-deception is a psychological necessity for her.

This quality of illusion horrifies Marlow. As he talks to her, he feels surrounded, menaced, by the wilderness. Her low voice is accompanied in his mind by whispers from the heart of darkness, the faint ring of incomprehensible words cried from afar. He feels panic as if he had blundered into a place of cruel and absurd mysteries not fit for a human being to behold.

In other words, he has journeyed once more towards the heart of darkness. The Intended puts out her arms as if after a retreating figure, and her gesture recalls that of Kurtz's mistress, when the steamboat was carrying him away. She is metamorphosed into the savage, for she too is a tragic figure, the prey of an incomprehensible passion. When Marlow lies to her about Kurtz's last words, he is astonished by her response:

> I heard a light sigh and then my heart stood still, stopped dead short by an exulting and terrible cry, by the cry of inconceivable triumph and of unspeakable pain.

The wilderness claims her, for her tragic ecstasy is Dionysiac in its fervour beyond the power of words. Her triumph and pain exemplify for Marlow "The horror! The horror!" at the end of his pilgrimage. He leaves her in her graveyard, where she can resist the darkness in her heart only because of his reverberating lie.

Heart of Darkness and the Gnostic Myth

Bruce Henricksen

The gnostic sects, which reached the height of their influence in the second century A.D., made a "tragic" response to the "comic" world view of orthodox Christianity, and while they did not become the dominant force in Christian thought, their teachings have continued to hold a muted resonance in our culture. It is this gnostic critique one hears in John Calvin's doctrines of election and innate depravity, and, ever since Nietzsche announced the death of God, the gnostic strain has sounded in our literature of alienation. The influence of gnostic thought on Blake, Shelley, Byron, and Melville has been established, and *Heart of Darkness,* with its somber tone, its mythic plot, and its dualistic tension between light and dark, is another and particularly strong example of the gnostic voice in our literature. While the question of whether *Heart of Darkness* is a tragedy has probably occurred to most readers, the many echoes in the novel of the gnostic myth and archetypes have gone unheard. Noticing these echoes will serve not only to suggest solutions to specific problems of interpretation, but also to provide a basis for a discussion of *Heart of Darkness* as tragedy.

It is somewhat misleading to say "the" gnostic myth, since each of the sects had a slightly different mythology and a different proximity to orthodox Christianity. There were many branches, and scholars have discovered many roots as well. Gnostic origins have been found in Hellenistic thought, in Judaism, and in Eastern influ-

From *Mosaic* 11, no. 4 (Summer 1978). © 1978 by the University of Manitoba Press.

ences such as Zoroastrianism and Buddhism. But all the sects shared a tragic view of the world as being intrinsically evil. The creator is himself evil, a god of darkness who is perhaps co-eternal with the transcendent god of light or who could have arisen from chaos as a response to the god of light. The myths differ; what is constant is the notion that forces of darkness were able, by using creation as a sort of prison, to entrap fragments of light emanating from the transcendent god. This god, who had nothing to do with creation, labors to retrieve the light, which has become lodged as "divine sparks" in the souls of men. Gnostic literature often refers to this god of light as "the alien," "the other," "the messenger," or "the kind stranger," emphasizing his lack of involvement in creation.

Gnostic myth, then, deals with the quest of this kind stranger, the goal of which is the return of something precious to its rightful place. In the less radical sects, Jesus, as the incarnate stranger, plays much the same role he does in orthodox Christianity. A pecularity of the gnostic myth, however, is the fallibility of the questing god; just as the sparks in men's souls have "forgotten" their divine identity, so the questing god runs the risk of forgetting himself and becoming enslaved by matter. Often he is portrayed as disguising himself in order to pass the evil spirits, or "eons," that inhabit the seven planetary spheres, but the disguise may bring about true loss of identity. Thus the problem of forgetfulness is always present as the principle opposing gnosis, symbolized usually by images of sleep or fog. Finally, the myth can be interpreted on more than one level, with the questing figure also representing man in his search for knowledge.

The entrapment of light by darkness is continually suggested by the imagery of *Heart of Darkness*. In the framing scene the few sparks of light are "stricken" by the night, and the motif is varied in the main plot with the ivory—the light which is the object of the quest—buried in the dark continent. Although the novel has been criticized for an overly facile, melancholy, and adjectival preoccupation with murky atmospheres, Conrad's confrontation with darkness has the integrity of a profound sensibility in the tradition of the *Beowulf* poet. In *Lord Jim,* particularly in the marvelously realized chapter after the jump, the question is one of conduct—how will man behave in the dark? In *Heart of Darkness* the demonic quality of darkness is established with images of mutilation, death, and hell— weapons of war, dead machinery, the grove of death (hell as parody of the garden), corpses, the river of forgetfulness, phantoms, devils, and fire—the sort of imagery that, in Northrop Frye's bureaucracy of types, occurs in "sixth-phase tragedy" and suggests the gnostic vision of the created world as intrinsically evil. It is also the kind of imagery Frye finds in ironic literature at the moment of its return to myth.

In this demonic world Kurtz is the alien god, or "kind stranger," who loses his identity during his quest, while ironically being idolized by the Russian and worshipped by the natives. Marlow repeats the quest "in the night of first ages." For him the problem of forgetfulness is symbolized as in the gnostic text *The Gospel of Truth* by images of sleep and fog. Some of what he knows about Kurtz he hears while dozing, and he sleeps again before his encounter with Kurtz; fog imagery also occurs shortly before Marlow meets Kurtz. Now, as storyteller, his problem is like that of recovering a dream, the reality is evasive, and he summarizes his position as alien when he says, "We live, as we dream—alone." The "life is a dream" notion, also found in *Lord Jim,* was a conventional vehicle for the gnostic critique of reality. The pressures on Marlow to forget parallel Kurtz's loss of identity, and his parallel to Kurtz as a god figure is indicated when the framing narrator calls him an "idol" and a "Buddha." But Marlow, at whatever psychic expense, preserves his identity.

This aspect of the plot, in which the first questing figure loses his identity and must be redeemed by a second, is central to gnostic myth and is not found in the other descent stories, such as Dante's *Inferno* and Virgil's *Aeneid,* to which the novel has been compared. Although the structure and imagery of *Heart of Darkness* are undeniably influenced by Dante, with Marlow even calling Africa an "inferno," it is a mistake to see the novel solely, or even primarily, in terms of a Dantesque vision. The cosmic drama of gnostic myth was silenced as heretical by the tradition in which Dante wrote, only to re-emerge in such figures as Blake, Melville, and Conrad. Conrad's references to traditional Christianity often contain elements of irony, and to the extent that his vision contains gnostic elements, he is Dante's rival, not his disciple.

Conrad's peculiarly gnostic plot structure, in which one questing figure must be redeemed by a second, derives from "The Hymn of the Pearl," found in the apocryphal *Acts of the Apostle Thomas.* Here the narrator has journeyed to Egypt (symbol of the material creation) in search of a pearl (symbol of divine light), but, having fallen into the dream of life, he has lost his identity and forgotten his mission, only to be saved by a second messenger sent from home. The following lines, spoken after he has realized his error, might well reflect the state of mind of Kurtz at the moment of his death:

> And when I was single and alone,
> A stranger to those with whom I dwelt
>
> . . . .
>
> . . . I put on a garb like theirs
> Lest they should recognize me because I had come from afar.
>
> . . . .
>
> I forgot that I was a son of kings,
> And I served their king;
> And I forgot the pearl,
> For which my parents had sent me,
> And by reason of the burden of their foods
> I lay in a deep sleep.

The speaker's brother comes with a letter from his parents, reminding him of his identity: "I remembered that I was a son of kings, / And my freedom longed for its own nature." The godlike Kurtz has come "equipped with the moral ideas," as Marlow says, and with "thunder and lightening" as his Russian "disciple" says, but he has eaten the food of the natives, perhaps, in demonic parody of the Eucharist, human flesh. He has forgotten his humanitarian purpose and is finally retrieved by his self-avowed brother, Marlow, and with the words "The horror! The horror!" sees his error. Marlow, as he seeks Kurtz, feels he is traveling on an "unknown planet" among "mean and greedy phantoms" like the eons of the gnostic descent myth who occupy the planetary spheres the alien god must pass by as he journeys through the creation that, to use Marlow's words again, is ruled by an "inscrutable" and "implacable" force. Marlow's estrangement from his world makes him fit Camus' definition of the absurd man, but the dualism involved in the definition is precisely the essence of gnosticism as well.

Commenting on "The Hymn of the Pearl" in a way that could also apply to *Heart of Darkness,* Jonas says that "the called sleeper is himself the messenger, the letter therefore a duplication of his role as he, on his part, duplicates that of the divine treasure he came to retrieve from the world. . . . [Here] we perceive some of the logic of that strain of eschatological symbolism which has been summarized in the expression, 'the savior saved.'" He goes on to say that "the interchangeability of subject and object of the mission, of savior and soul, of Prince and Pearl, is the key to the true meaning of the poem, and to gnostic eschatology in general." And certainly the relationship between Kurtz and Marlow is the key to Conrad's novel.

In tone, imagery, and plot, *Heart of Darkness* reveals a gnostic attitude and tells a gnostic story, the plight of its principal characters being a manifestation of the universal laws found in gnostic eschatology. Conrad transforms the gnostic myth into the historical realities of his time and into the language—the mists and melancholy—of post-Symbolism. While looking back to gnostic elements in Blake and Melville, the preciseness of Conrad's transformation, or "homeomorph" (to use Hugh Kenner's term), looks forward to Pound's poetry and to Joyce's homeomorph of *The Odyssey*.

The questing god in his two roles is the prototype of the Kurtz-Marlow relationship. But their relationship also implies the differences between the hedonistic branch of gnosticism and the ascetic branch. The hedonistic sects taught that, since redemption is not a matter of forgiveness of sins but of election and release from fate, abusing the body is a reasonable way to scorn creation. This logic suggests Hellenistic influences, while looking ahead to the Reformation question as to whether the elect are above scriptural law. The ascetic sects, influenced more by Buddhism, scorned creation by renunciation. The *Pistis-Sophia,* a principal text of the Valentinian gnostics, severely criticizes the Ophites for practising Serpent worship—the Ophites believed that the serpent who offered man knowledge was the "kind stranger" in disguise. Kurtz, slithering through the grass toward his final rendezvous, is of their camp. Epiphanius, writing in the fourth century, refers to "unspeakably foul rites and practices" of the Ophites. This, rhetorical vagueness and all, is Marlow's language.

Marlow's celibacy also aligns him with the ascetics, who believed procreation to be a device of the evil god to keep the divine sparks perpetually entrapped in matter. Furthermore, he shares the ascetic's notion that too much introspection is dangerous because of the risk of deepening one's involvement in the creation one should renounce. He is glad to have his work to occupy his mind, and as he navigates he sees only the surface signs, "The inner truth is hidden—luckily, luckily." He of course sees his entire story as an inner journey, but it was not voluntary—it was an ordeal and a "nightmare." And this avoidance of the inner truth of things, which prepares us for the lie to Kurtz's Intended, explains Marlow's lack of interest in the underlying economic and political causes for the exploitation of Africa. Conrad himself, in his correspondence with Robert Cunninghame Graham, undercuts Graham's political optimism by arguing that an awareness of the "negating force" at the heart of existence renders any rational political movement impossible. Finally, Marlow's habits of renunciation are underscored in the framing scene when he says he has no more interest in world travel, "the glamor's off," and when the narrator actually describes him as a Buddha.

If Kurtz and Marlow can be seen as types of the lost and the redeeming gods, and also as representatives of hedonistic and ascetic gnosticism respectively, the two female figures in the novel also correspond to aspects of gnostic myth, in which there is a female figure aligned with the side of light and another with darkness. On the side of light is the "First Woman," who stands for the Holy Spirit or for Sophia; sometimes she is called a sister, sometimes a bride—in any case, reunion with her occurs after successful completion of the quest. Jonas calls her "a figure of light who comes to meet the dying." She is embodied in Kurtz's Intended, who is luminous in a dwelling described in imagery suggesting a funeral home. The intentions of the evil god are personified in a rival female figure who represents matter and also, since procreation is a device of entrapment, sexuality. She is embodied in the Black Princess. These types have found a permanent place in romance. To the Red Crosse Knight they are Una and Duessa, and Arthur has his Intended in the Faerie Queene herself. They recur as the light and dark heroines of Victorian romance—"the lady of duty and the lady of pleasure," as Frye calls them. And if, as Frye believes, the Christian myth as found in the Bible is the prototype of romance, then it is appropriate that a gnostic tragedy should involve not only a romantic failure but a generic pattern of failed romance.

Seeing the two women in terms of these mythic types will probably not put to rest the question of Marlow's lie, but the lie makes sense in the gnostic context. To tell the Intended the truth would be, despite Stein, to immerse her needlessly in the destructive element of creation; that is, to perpetuate verbally the "truth" of the evil world, like perpetuating the human race itself, plays into the hands of the negating force, but to treat the "truth" as though it does not exist is to act for the liberation of the light. As Marlow says of women, "We must help them to stay in that beautiful world of their own, lest ours get worse." We recall the inadequacy of "facts" at Jim's trial as well as Conrad's characterization of a man like Chester, who, with no blue guitar, sees things as they are. And elsewhere in *Lord Jim* Marlow, as storyteller, argues for the higher value of "the truth disclosed in a moment of illusion" as opposed to mere factual truth. Marlow's lie is the ultimate act of renunciation on the part of an ascetic who scorns the created world, and it is the ultimate service to the higher truth beyond creation. The ultimate truth is served by the penultimate lie. An appreciation of this point depends on remembering that the god of light is, to the gnostic view, entirely "other," an alien to the laws governing creation. The gnostics, in fact, inherited the Buddhist notion that creation should be viewed as a dream from which one seeks release. In this spirit Marlow dismisses the "truth" about Kurtz, thus protecting the light of innocence that radiates from his Intended—and thus fulfilling his mission as saviour figure, truly becoming the "kind stranger" of gnostic myth.

I have suggested that Conrad had the gnostic myth consciously in mind in *Heart of Darkness*. This possibility is reinforced by the fact that a number of works on gnosticism were in print that Conrad could have known and by the general interest in comparative religion, folklore, and anthropology in the years prior to the novel's publication, particularly Frazer's analyses of the mythical content of primitive drama. It would be interesting to find external evidence to verify Conrad's intention in this regard, but it is not essential to know what was in Conrad's mind—only what came out of it. We can assume, with Frye, that all of literature is a memory bank in which a finite number of myths and archetypes recur at various points and in various guises along the curve of literary history and that each new work "is born into an already existing order of words, and is typical of the structure of poetry to which it is attached." In what follows I will touch on the "attachment" of *Heart of Darkness* to the structure of tragedy. I. A. Richards has said, "Tragedy is only possible to a mind which is for the moment agnostic or Manichean." It would take us too far afield to argue the complex question of whether or not tragedy is compatible with a Christian world view, but if there is truth in Richards's assertion it is not surprising that at some point a tragedy should emerge with a number of precise and apparently studied parallels to Manichean, or gnostic, myth.

That the plot of *Heart of Darkness* is similar in kind to those of Shakespeare's tragedies is clear enough. Kurtz is a somewhat ironic version of the "high mimetic" hero—just how ironic is unclear, being shrouded, like Jim, in too many fogs and mists. Such is his enigma. At any rate, he is an aspiring mind who falls and is isolated from society, the fall being related to a fault in his character and both fall and fault being of a magnitude to arouse pity and fear. While on the anagogic level Kurtz is a type of questing god, on the level of a particular bank and shoal of time he is a sort of Macbeth displaced into the power struggles of the late nineteenth century. As such, he is also a parody of Matthew Arnold's man of culture, obviously lacking the spiritual authority Arnold assumed accompanied "culture." Kurtz's culture, like the principles Marlow talks about, flies off at the first good shake, leaving an unaccommodated man who gives the lie not only to the Arnoldian notion of the saving powers of culture but to Rousseau's optimism concerning the nature of man. In fact, while challenging the traditional certainties of the nineteenth century, Conrad's portrayal of Kurtz's inability to live outwardly from a firm core of being, from a "deliberate belief" as Marlow puts it, anticipates with amazing accuracy one of the most prevalent symptoms that psychotherapists have encountered in recent decades. While too exceptional to precisely fit Riesman's definition of the "other-directed" person, Kurtz, like the members of the lonely crowd, possesses a "civilized" personality that is only veneer. Conrad's anticipation of Riesman is even more startling when we recall the carefully scrubbed and starched accountant Marlow meets at the outer station—an "inner-directed" man who has so entirely and unquestioningly internalized exterior values as to preclude ever having to face a crisis of identity. Thus, while creating in the fall of Kurtz a traditional tragic pattern, Conrad is also addressing himself to the kinds of identity crises peculiar to our times.

Murray Krieger says Kurtz is like Kierkegaard's knight of faith, having launched himself, like Abraham, beyond the bounds of the ethical; Marlow, on the other hand, rests in the ethical, experiencing only vicariously the fear and trembling of the man who is entirely free. Krieger's argument is provocative, but I object to it on the grounds that Kurtz never possessed that firm core of being which is the "self" the Kierkegaardian knight of faith launches. Kurtz's tragedy is precisely his *failure* to be free in a post-Kierkegaardian age. Furthermore, Krieger's assessment of Marlow is not entirely consistent: at times he makes Marlow simply a spokesman for the ethical, but elsewhere he says Marlow's position is "strangely paradoxical" in that his inner strength enables him to grasp the very principles he has scorned as useless. But certainly there is no real problem here. What Marlow scorns is the man who holds principles without ever knowing why; his own adherence to the ethical is the commitment of a man confronting lived experience who truly possesses an inner self. Marlow identifies more with Kurtz than with the thoughtless members of the ethical society and their demonic parodies at the Central Station. He is a sort of fulcrum, delicately balancing the claims of a shattered ethical, or classical, society against, if Krieger is right, the dreadful alienation of a Kierkegaardian world view, or, alternately, against the inner emptiness of the lonely crowd. At any rate, it is in terms such as these that Marlow, as latter day gnostic initiate, comes to understand the forms through which the forces of darkness work in the modern world for the entrapment of being. In other words, the novel examines a contemporary form of the gnostic problem of the entrapment of being by darkness, and it does this via a traditional tragic plot.

Kurtz's journey beyond the ethical recalls Macbeth, but he is really like Macbeth and the Weird Sisters in one, breaking with Dionysian energy (or "will," the term Schopenhauer inherited from the Renaissance) the bonds of Apollonian order while threatening our sense of reality with his deathly other-worldiness. The gnostic vision of *Macbeth* climaxes with the "Tomorrow and tomorrow" speech while *Heart of Darkness* climaxes with the marvelously enigmatic "The horror! The horror!"—both speeches deliver oracular truths that echo the elegaic lament of Greek tragedy. But while Malcolm and Macduff emerge, after the prayer that ends act 3, as the instruments of divine grace, Conrad's plot does not mitigate its gnostic vision with a comfortable and orthodox reconciliation. Malcolm reestablishes an order assumed to be natural, but Marlow protects society from the truth about nature (human and cosmic) with his lie. The gnostic vision does not end with Kurtz's death: it is confirmed by it. Like Horatio, Marlow lives to tell the story, but, still the fulcrum, he tells it in two versions—one for the world at large and one for the initiates who are, presumably, ready for *gnosis*. Marlow's pride in his special knowledge is reflected in remarks such as, "You can't understand. How could you?—with solid pavement under your feet." His need to tell two versions recalls the compromises such writers as Dickens and Hardy had to negotiate between the "true" story and the story their audiences could accept, but in terms of the present thesis we can see Marlow's behavior as reflecting the elitism of the original gnostics.

Although the fall of Kurtz creates the tragic pattern, Marlow is at least as important a character as Horatio. Therefore it is interesting to find Frye saying that the end of *Hamlet* conveys a strong sense of it having been Horatio's story. When Horatio actually gets around to telling the story, the stage is no longer the boards of the Globe but the consciousness of the man who was there and who therefore attracts a large share of the interest. The techniques of the first person novel allowed Conrad to realize a notion Shakespeare seems to have at the end of *Hamlet* concerning the true locus of the story.

Marlow, too, is archetypal. As our "Buddha," he is one who knows; he has experienced the shattering of the ethical and the terror of freedom, and his function aboard the *Nellie* is priestly. The ship is a microcosm, and the water on which it floats, and over which the story is told, is rich in mythic resonance. It is Conrad's own destructive element as well as the water over which one passes into death, but it also carries associations with the womb and birth, raising the question of the power of the word to germinate a redeemed society. And if this is the ultimate function of the one who speaks, we find in Marlow echoes of Moses, who is first encountered adrift on the water, and Jesus, who walked on the water and returned from hell. Marlow's story, which occurred in "the night of first ages," embodies, like all religious tales and rituals, a recollection of an event assumed to have been of cosmic importance to the "tribe" (one imagines a version told by Marlow's African counterpart). The knowledge Marlow possesses is Manichean, of a world that can only be saved by exercising mental reservation to create "a saving illusion." But Marlow's story is not only priestly, containing the cosmic knowledge of the tribe, it is also personal, and he compares it often to a dream, that psychic phenomenon in which realities of the dreamer's own inner nature are symbolized. The story is also an inner journey, and the need to suppress the story from society in Belgium corresponds to the censorship mechanism of forgetfulness on the psychic level that causes Marlow's narrative occasionally to break down, frustrating his attempts to remember. These observations confirm the view of the story as myth, for it is in myth that ritual and dream, or social vision and psychic vision, merge.

While recalling the traditional myth of gnosticism and the traditional literary form of tragedy, *Heart of Darkness* is a profound evocation of the particular forms of darkness confronting our own age. Man, as he labors to define himself, never does so directly, but always by recapturing the past, and each expression of the individual talent derives its being and nourishment from past forms. By possessing the past on, and in terms of, the horizon of his own time, man, whom Nietzsche has called the yet-to-be-determined animal, comes to know himself and to project his destiny.

*H*eart of Darkness

R. A. Gekoski

Heart of Darkness (1900) is one of Conrad's most ambiguous and difficult stories, a tale which has captivated critics with its profuse imagery and philosophical and psychological suggestiveness. It seems almost deliberately constructed in order to provide employment to teachers, critics, and editors of literary casebooks. There are as many "readings" of the story as its Mr Kurtz has tusks of ivory—many of them gained by similarly "unsound method." Its imagery has been described in detail, resonances from Dante, Milton, the Bible, the *Upanishads,* invoked; its philosophical position is argued variously to be Schopenhauerian, Nietzschean, nihilist, existentialist, or Christian; its psychology, Freudian, Jungian, Adlerian, or (more recently) Laingian. That the story has been so comprehensively "understood" would have surprised Conrad, who was concerned that it might prove elusive even to his most sympathetic readers; he wrote to Cunninghame Graham at the time that the story was being serialized:

> There are two more instalments in which the idea is so wrapped up in secondary notions that You—even You!— may miss it. And also you must remember that I don't start with an abstract notion. I start with definite images and as their rendering is true some little effect is produced.

In *Heart of Darkness,* Conrad takes his deepest look into the human condition, and comes to perhaps his most pessimistic conclusions on

From *Conrad: The Moral World of the Novelist.* © 1978 by R. A. Gekoski. Harper & Row, 1978.

the various and incompatible pressures that can be imposed on the human spirit. The readings that the story has given rise to are a testimonial not only to the power and range of its concerns, but to their elusiveness. I shall try, in this chapter, to locate the "idea" that Conrad tells us lies behind the story, and to discuss at some length the "secondary notions" with which it is associated.

I have argued that *The Nigger of the "Narcissus"* treats, in microcosmic terms, the threat to social equilibrium implicit in a recognition of the ultimate futility of life. *Heart of Darkness* focuses on a similar problem (the image of "darkness" echoing the resonance of "blackness" in the previous story), although here what is threatened is not only the group, but also the individual. Whereas Conrad had conveniently circumvented the difficulty of his inadequate protagonists in choosing, for the hero of *The Nigger of the "Narcissus"*, the entire crew of a ship, in *Heart of Darkness* the problem is solved—not once, but twice: we not only have the figure of Mr Kurtz, the "universal genius," but also that of Marlow, in a more complex and morally dynamic role than he previously played in "Youth." We cannot, in fact, adequately understand *Heart of Darkness* if we do not begin by considering in structural terms the relationship that it establishes between Kurtz and Marlow.

We must begin by recognizing that the story is as much about Marlow as about Kurtz. This may seem obvious, but it is nevertheless true that many critics have read *Heart of Darkness* as if Marlow were simply a means of getting us *to* Kurtz. Such a reading may be implicit in F. R. Leavis's suggestion that "it is not for nothing that *Heart of Darkness,* a predominantly successful tale, is told by the captain of the steamboat—told from that specific and concretely realised point of view." Such a view fails to account for the tension that Conrad maintains between different points of view, and finally forces the critic to posit artistic flaws (Leavis objects to Conrad's "making a virtue out of not knowing what he means" and to the "bad patch" in which Marlow visits Kurtz's Intended) where actually there are virtues. Considered solely as a study of the disintegration of Mr Kurtz, the story is simply a bad one—overlong, digressive, and poorly structured: of its 117 pages, fully twenty-five are set outside Africa, and of those dealing with Africa a great many contain no mention of Kurtz. Indeed, Kurtz's crucial role in the tale lies in his symbolic importance: in the representative quality of his history, in his role as a final incarnation of the darkness itself, and as a potential aspect of Marlow's own self.

We are made aware of Kurtz's symbolic role through the recurrent dream-imagery, which locates him as a phantom in Marlow's dream, as a "nightmare" from which Marlow only barely manages to awake. This is clear in several places in the story, particularly in the passage in which Marlow turns in frustration to his sceptical audience aboard the ship moored quietly in the Thames:

> "I became in an instant as much of a pretence as the rest of the bewitched pilgrims. This simply because I had a notion it would somehow be of help to that Kurtz whom at the time I did not see—you understand. He was just a word for me. I did not see the man in the name any more than you do. Do you see him? Do you see the story? Do you see anything? It seems to me I am trying to tell you a dream—making a vain attempt, because no relation of a dream can convey the dream-sensation, that commingling of absurdity, surprise, and bewilderment in a tremor of struggling revolt, that notion of being captured by the incredible, which is of the very essence of dreams . . ."
>
> He was silent for a while.
>
> ". . . No, it is impossible; it is impossible to convey the life-sensation of any given epoch of one's existence—that which makes its truth, its meaning—its subtle and penetrating essence. We live, as we dream—alone . . ."

Insofar, then, as *Heart of Darkness* is to attempt the impossible—to render the meaning of a dream—we have to remember the context in which the dream is placed. The tale unfolds in layers: first, we have the anonymous "I" who serves as narrator aboard a ship in the Thames, in the company of the same group who formed the cast of "Youth"—the lawyer, the accountant, the director, and Marlow; inside this outer frame there is Charley Marlow himself, telling another of his "inconclusive" stories; within Marlow's tale, too, there are several recognizable layers, for his trip to Africa is framed at the beginning and end by important visits to Brussels, and even his time in Africa is spent on that essential voyage—the trip up the river to pick up Kurtz, and back again. Like a concentric series of ripples caused by a stone thrown into the water, we are presented with an interrelated series of personal and social contexts, all of them affected by the impact of the central agent, Mr Kurtz.

To begin with Marlow. His decision to travel up the Congo is presented to us as the romantic aspiration of a man seeking after the "glamour" of the mysterious, acting out a childhood (perhaps a childish) wish to seek out "that blank space of delightful mystery" that deepest Africa represented on the maps of the time. He finds, at the offices of the steamship company in Brussels, an atmosphere reeking with images of death, and is sensitive enough to note the "ominous" atmosphere; he is far from deterred, however, and leaves Brussels feeling himself involved in a "commonplace" affair. But it is not long before Marlow's superficial uneasiness gives way to a deeper sense of foreboding. Even during his voyage along the African coast, he is already describing his experience as "a weary pilgrimage amongst hints for nightmares," a realistic detail with which Conrad is quietly building a major theme of the story. The sight of the French man-of-war, anchored offshore and casually firing again and again into the murky interior of the jungle, is Marlow's first hint of the dark purposelessness ("There was a touch of insanity in the proceeding") with which he is to be confronted. The first white man that Marlow meets at the Central Station is the accountant, a figure ludicrously well groomed amidst the sordid surroundings. Marlow is drawn to the man immediately:

> Yes; I respected his collars, his vast cuffs, his brushed hair. His appearance was certainly that of a hairdresser's dummy; but in the great demoralisation of the land he kept up his appearance. That's backbone. His starched collars and got-up shirt-fronts were achievements of character. . . . Thus this man had verily accomplished something. And he was devoted to his books, which were in apple-pie order.

In sharp contrast to the natty, but efficient, figure of the accountant stand those of the manager and brickmaker of the station. The chief virtue of the former—to which he apparently owes his relatively prosperous position—is his good health. Marlow, appalled by the insensitive immorality of the man, muses:

> Perhaps there was nothing within him. Such a suspicion made one pause—for out there there were no external checks. Once when various tropical diseases had laid low almost every "agent" in the station, he was heard to say, "Men who come out here should have no entrails."

This thematic association of success with immorality (imaged, as in *The Nigger of the "Narcissus,"* by personal emptiness) is repeated with reference to the brickmaker:

> It seemed to me that if I tried I could poke my forefinger through him, and would find nothing inside but a little loose dirt, maybe.

The failure of these men may lie in some internal deficiency, but it is manifested in the fact that they do not work:

> They beguiled the time by backbiting and intriguing against each other in a foolish kind of way. There was an air of plotting about that station, but nothing came of it, of course. It was as unreal as everything else—as the philanthropic pretence of the whole concern, as their talk, as their government, as their show of work. The only real feeling was a desire to get appointed to a trading-post where ivory was to be had, so that they could earn percentages.

Marlow is thus disturbed both by the immorality of the manager, brickmaker and "pilgrims" who soon join them, and by their "unreality" (a word repeated several times). This is an odd conjunction; although there is an undeniable air of evil about the Central Station, it cannot dispel the foolish emptiness of the existence led there. It was, of course, from a similar conjunction of evil and absurdity that Conrad produced the gruesome amusement of the murder in "An Outpost of Progress." In *Heart of Darkness,* the same point is nicely conveyed in a series of images which link evil with insignificance: there is a "fiendish" sound about the station, but it is only the buzzing of the flies; the manager is called a "devil," but he is a "flabby devil"; the brickmaker may be Mephistopheles, but he is a "papier-mâché Mephistopheles." It is out of this context of greed and ennui that Marlow's initial interest in Kurtz develops. "He is a prodigy. . . . He is an emissary of pity, and science, and progress, and devil knows what else." Intrigued by the brickmaker's description of Kurtz, and finding a solid satisfaction in the daily work of repairing his damaged steamboat, Marlow is able to combat the corrosive effects of life in the wilderness. He begins to see Kurtz as having a certain symbolic importance: "I was curious to see whether this man, who had come out equipped with moral ideas of some sort, would climb to the top after all and how he would set about his work when there."

At this point Marlow begins to make a distinction between two types of "reality," a subject upon which his thoughts have turned since calling the men of the Central Station "unreal." There is, first of all, the reality that Marlow assigns to the mundane efficiency of his everyday tasks, which is later to be described as the "surface-truth" of life, and associated with the saving illusion of the work ethic. But Marlow is now becoming aware of an insidious force which he locates in (and as) the jungle—though the symbolic nature of that "darkness" is still being developed—which is also "real." The distinction between these two, apparently contradictory, senses of "reality," and their contrast to the "unreality" of the Central Station, underlies the following passage:

> I went to work the next day, turning, so to speak, my back on that station. In that way only it seemed to me I could keep my hold on the redeeming facts of life. Still, one must look about sometimes; and then I saw this station, these men strolling aimlessly about in the sunshine of the yard. I asked myself sometimes what it all meant. They wandered here and there with their absurd long staves in their hands, like a lot of faithless pilgrims bewitched inside a rotten fence. The word "ivory" rang in the air, was whispered, was sighed. You would think they were praying to it. A taint of imbecile rapacity blew through it all, like a whiff from some corpse. By Jove! I've never seen anything so unreal in my life! And outside, the silent wilderness surrounding this cleared speck on the earth struck me as something great and invincible, like evil or truth, waiting patiently for the passing away of this fantastic invasion.

From this point in the story onward, it is to be the tension between these two types of reality—between the reality of ethical imperative and the metaphysical reality of "the darkness"—that is of crucial interest.

After three months' delay, Marlow at last sets off upriver with the aim of relieving Kurtz at the Inner Station. His voyage is now, clearly, both a literal and a symbolic journey:

> Going up that river was like travelling back to the earliest beginnings of the world, when vegetation rioted on the

> earth and the big trees were kings. . . . There were mo-
> ments when one's past came back to one, as it will some-
> times when you have not a moment to spare to yourself;
> but it came in the shape of an unrestful and noisy dream,
> remembered with wonder amongst the overwhelming re-
> alities of this strange world of plants, and water, and si-
> lence. And this stillness of life did not in the least resemble
> a peace. It was the stillness of an implacable force brooding
> over an inscrutable intention. It looked at you with venge-
> ful aspect. I got used to it afterwards; I did not see it any
> more; I had no time.

Let us stop to ask the obvious questions. Does "It was the stillness of an implacable force brooding over an inscrutable intention" simply strain language to the breaking point?—are we to conclude (with F. R. Leavis) that Conrad is intent on "making a virtue out of not knowing what he means"?

It appears that Conrad is attempting to render some force which exists not only outside, but also inside, the self—a force which will ultimately constitute a threat to Marlow's psychic equilibrium when it comes to be embodied by Mr Kurtz. Its nature is oxymoronic: it is dreamlike, but nevertheless terrifyingly real; it is "implacable," but "inscrutable"—that is, incapable of being resisted, but incapable of being identified; it is overwhelming, but can be, if not overcome, at least resisted. It is not enough to locate in this passage the typical late-Victorian shock and horror at the universal human capacity for depravity. For Conrad, the "horror" cannot be assigned to the fallen nature of man; indeed, our inner darkness simply enacts that of a universe not merely indifferent, but, here, positively malignant. Whether one wishes to invoke Freud's id, Jung's shadow (a term explicitly used to describe Kurtz), or Nietzsche's Will to Power, what must be understood is that the "darkness" is now both external and potentially internal—and that its full fruition constitutes a danger to the equilibrium of the self. This darkness, in its symbolic sense, is not only overwhelmingly powerful, but virtually unknowable, because it almost never manifests itself in unmediated experience. Marlow is sharply aware that he is trying to express the inexpressible; his rhetorical strategy is to invoke its inexpressibility—he constantly turns to his audience, challenging them with the fact that they are simply not equipped with a depth of experience sufficient properly to understand what he is trying to say. In this oblique way, Conrad is able to suggest that which, by its very nature, can be known (except to the exceptional man) only in timorous half-glances.

As the steamship creeps onwards towards Kurtz, the darkness which is externally manifested in the jungle, and internally at some point deep within the self, becomes an increasing threat to Marlow's stability—an ultimate "reality" seeking to escape both from and into the depths of his being. The process is virtually irresistible, as Marlow has previously suggested with the phrase "the fascination of the abomination"; his narrative conveys an impression of astonishment:

> The steamer toiled along slowly on the edge of a black and incomprehensible frenzy. The prehistoric man was cursing us, praying to us, welcoming us—who could tell? We were cut off from the comprehension of our surroundings; we glided past like phantoms, wondering and secretly appalled, as sane men would be before an enthusiastic outbreak in a madhouse. We could not understand because we were too far and could not remember, because we were travelling in the night of first ages, of those ages that are gone, leaving hardly a sign—and no memories.
>
> The earth seemed unearthly. We are accustomed to look upon the shackled form of a conquered monster, but there—there you could look at a thing monstrous and free. It was unearthly, and the men were—No, they were not inhuman. Well, you know, that was the worst of it—this suspicion of their not being inhuman. It would come slowly to one. They howled and leaped, and spun, and made horrid faces: but what thrilled you was just the thought of their humanity—like yours—the thought of your remote kinship with this wild and passionate uproar. Ugly. Yes, it was ugly enough; but if you were man enough you would admit to yourself that there was in you just the faintest trace of a response to the terrible frankness of that noise, a dim suspicion of there being a meaning in it which you—you so remote from the night of first ages—could comprehend. And why not? The mind of man is capable of anything—because everything is in it, all the past as well as all the future. What was there after all? Joy, fear, sorrow, devotion, valour, rage—who can tell?—but truth—truth stripped of its cloak of time. Let the fool

gape and shudder—the man knows, and can look on without a wink. But he must at least be as much of a man as those on the shore. He must meet that truth with his own true stuff—with his own inborn strength. Principles won't do. Acquisitions, clothes, pretty rags—rags that would fly off at the first good shake. No; you want a deliberate belief. An appeal to me in this fiendish row—is there? Very well; I hear; I admit, but I have a voice, too, and for good or evil mine is the speech that cannot be silenced. Of course, a fool, what with sheer fright and fine sentiments, is always safe. Who's that grunting? You wonder I didn't go ashore for a howl and a dance? Well, no—I didn't. Fine sentiments, you say? Fine sentiments, be hanged! I had no time. I had to mess about with white-lead and strips of woollen blanket helping to put bandages on those leaky steam-pipes—I tell you. I had to watch the steering, and circumvent those snags, and get the tin-pot along by hook or by crook. There was surface-truth enough in these things to save a wiser man.

There are several important distinctions here. First, that it is only the "man" (as opposed to the "fool") who is susceptible to the atavistic appeal of savage reversion. The fool will not respond to the call of the savages because he is not aware of its truth, because he has shielded himself from the darkness latent within his own breast. The "man," on the other hand, is aware of the "common humanity" that links him with the "black and incomprehensible frenzy" of the darkness, with the savage and primitive forces within himself. A second distinction, however, exists between the "man" who, though aware of the appeal of the darkness, resists it, and the "man" who succumbs—that is, between Marlow and Kurtz. This is further related to a vague and unsatisfactory distinction between principles and beliefs: "Principles won't do . . . you want a deliberate belief." Perhaps the two can be distinguished—*Nostromo* tries to do so—but in this context they cannot. We remember Marlow's earlier words:

The conquest of the earth, which mostly means the taking it away from those who have a different complexion or slightly flatter noses than ourselves, is not a pretty thing when you look into it too much. What redeems it is the idea only. An idea at the back of it; not a sentimental pre-

tence but an idea; and an unselfish belief in the idea—
something you can set up, and bow down before, and offer
a sacrifice to.

Beliefs can become fetishes, as men (like Kurtz) can become gods.
Neither process is salutary.

But there is something more; Marlow finds his security not only
in the "surface-truth" of his daily endeavour, but he is also able to
call upon some "inborn inner strength." Either a man has such
strength, or he doesn't. Those described in terms of hollowness—
the manager, the brickmaker, the "pilgrims," and, it seems, Kurtz—
do not have it; the accountant, the cannibals aboard Marlow's steamship (a neat ironic twist), and Marlow himself, are the fortunate pos-
sessors of this asset.

It isn't long before Marlow is telling us that "as to superstitions,
beliefs, and what you may call principles, they are less than chaff in
a breeze." Perhaps this indicates that his previous distinction between
principles and beliefs was halfhearted, but it also prepares us for
what is to come—for the time when only that nebulous "inborn
strength" will allow a man to fight off the call of the darkness. In his
description of the agony of that voyage, Marlow asks his listeners:
"Don't you know the devilry of lingering starvation, its exasperating
torment, its black thoughts, its sombre and brooding ferocity? Well,
I do. It takes a man all his inborn strength to fight hunger properly."
We are dealing here with a "hunger" that is not only of the body, but
of the soul (hence the repetition of "all his inborn strength")—a hunger which Conrad associates first with physical starvation, then links
to the "appetite" for ivory, and finally extends to a general and overpowering sense of physical and mental desire, suggested in Kurtz's
"weirdly voracious aspect."

Chapter 3 begins with Marlow's encounter with Kurtz's Russian
disciple—an incident of some importance in delaying, and setting
the tone for, Marlow's approaching meeting with Kurtz. The Russian sees Kurtz as a noble soul, entitled by his innate qualities to
the magisterial enactment of his own desires. This view—balancing
that of Kurtz as a merely lawless ivory hunter—places him (in
Nietzsche's phrase) "beyond good and evil"—"You can't judge Mr
Kurtz as you would an ordinary man"—and implicitly poses one of
the story's major questions: how *is* Kurtz to be judged? The desire
to answer this question underlies Marlow's anticipation of the much

delayed meeting with Kurtz, who has just returned from a long journey with another gigantic lot of ivory. This "appetite for more ivory," which we have seen to be linked to a less easily satisfied spiritual hunger, is soon associated with the colour of the skeleton heads with which Kurtz adorns his house. Marlow is not so much shocked by the sight of the heads, as by what they reveal about the state of mind of Mr Kurtz:

> They only showed that Mr Kurtz lacked restraint in the gratification of his various lusts, that there was something wanting in him—some small matter which, when the pressing need arose, could not be found under his magnificent eloquence. Whether he knew of this deficiency himself I can't say. I think the knowledge came to him at last— only at the very last. But the wilderness had found him out early, and had taken on him a terrible vengeance for the fantastic invasion. I think it had whispered to him things about himself which he did not know, things of which he had no conception till he took counsel with this great solitude—and the whisper had proved irresistibly fascinating. It echoed loudly within him because he was hollow at the core.

The symbolic association of the ivory with the heads outside Kurtz's house is then extended until it suggests the very essence of Kurtz himself; Marlow's first description of the man neatly combines the two images:

> I could see the cage of his ribs all astir, the bones of his arm waving. It was as though an animated image of death carved out of old ivory had been shaking its hand with menaces at a motionless crowd of men made of dark and glittering bronze. I saw him open his mouth wide—it gave him a weirdly voracious aspect, as though he had wanted to swallow all the air, all the earth, all the men before him.

But we are never to know the secret of Mr Kurtz's degradation, nor the nature of the "abominable satisfactions" in which he has immersed himself. This is only mildly frustrating, certainly not an artistic failure. Nothing is so uninteresting (as any reader of Sade will know) as a detailed description of abominable satisfactions.

The manager of the Central Station, impressed yet disturbed by the huge amounts of ivory that Kurtz has collected, expresses to Marlow the opinion that the ivory trade will be ruined by Kurtz's "unsound method." This phrase, glibly bypassing all of the unspeakable evils which Kurtz has perpetrated, appals Marlow. It is at this point that his identification with Kurtz first becomes explicit, for in his assertion that Kurtz is nevertheless "a remarkable man" he chooses to side with him against the manager and his fellow "fools." The decision is embodied in the phrase "a choice of nightmares," by which Marlow attempts to justify his sympathy with the full-blooded egoism of Kurtz rather than with the nasty equivocation of the "pilgrims" and their like. But really he is responding not so much to Kurtz as to what Kurtz may be said to represent:

> I had turned to the wilderness really, not to Mr Kurtz, who, I was ready to admit, was as good as buried. And for a moment it seemed to me as if I also were buried in a vast grave full of unspeakable secrets. I felt an intolerable weight oppressing my breast, the smell of the damp earth, the unseen presence of victorious corruption, the darkness of an impenetrable night.

The threat that Kurtz represents becomes increasingly real to Marlow as his knowledge of the man (and, by extension, of himself), and his distance from the saving grace of everyday work, increase. He recognizes that only he can seek Kurtz out after his remarkable escape:

> I did not betray Mr Kurtz—it was ordered I should never betray him—it was written I should be loyal to the nightmare of my choice. I was anxious to deal with this shadow by myself alone,—and to this day I don't know why I was so jealous of sharing with anyone the peculiar blackness of that experience.

Like that of James Wait at the end of *The Nigger of the "Narcissus,"* Kurtz's role is now almost purely symbolic: he, too, is a "blackness" that must somehow be resisted.

As Marlow blindly searches the jungles, recognizing (perhaps a bit conveniently) that he is confusing the beating of drums with that of his heart, he comes upon an ill and desperate Kurtz crawling back towards the savage enclave of which he is the adored leader. This ultimate struggle of will between Marlow and Kurtz can easily be misunderstood. Jocelyn Baines, for instance, asserts that Marlow "is even able to wrest Kurtz from the grasp of the wilderness when he is drawn back to it," which greatly oversimplifies the scene. Marlow does make the statement ("You will be lost . . . utterly lost") that sways Kurtz in his tortured conflict, but it is Kurtz alone who finally resists the virtually irresistible call of the darkness, and allows himself to be led back to "civilization." Had he chosen to "make a row," Kurtz would have been heard, and rescued, by the natives. But he does not do so, and this is perhaps the basis of his final triumph, and of Marlow's fidelity to his memory.

In his description of their struggle, Marlow gives us the key to the puzzling and terrifying character of Kurtz:

> I had to deal with a being to whom I could not appeal in the name of anything high or low. I had, even like the niggers, to invoke him—himself—his own exalted and incredible degradation. There was nothing either above or below him, and I knew it. He had kicked himself loose of the earth. Confound the man! he had kicked the very earth to pieces. He was alone, and I before him did not know whether I stood on the ground or floated in the air. I've been telling you what we said—repeating the phrases we pronounced—but what's the good? They were common everyday words—the familiar, vague sounds exchanged on every waking day of life. But what of that? They had behind them, to my mind, the terrific suggestiveness of words heard in dreams, of phrases spoken in nightmares. Soul! If anybody has ever struggled with a soul, I am the man. And I wasn't arguing with a lunatic either. Believe me or not, his intelligence was perfectly clear—concentrated, it is true, upon himself with horrible intensity, yet clear; and therein was my only chance—barring of course, the killing him there and then, which wasn't so good, on account of the unavoidable noise. But his soul was mad. Being alone in the wilderness, it had looked within itself, and, by heavens! I tell you, it had gone mad. I had—for my sins, I suppose—to go through the ordeal of looking into it myself. No eloquence could have been so withering to one's belief in mankind as his final burst of sincerity. He struggled with himself, too. I saw it,—I heard it. I saw the

> inconceivable mystery of a soul that knew no restraint, no
> faith, and no fear, yet struggling blindly with itself.

Several phrases early in the passage—"a being to whom I could not appeal in the name of anything high or low," "There was nothing either above or below him," "He had kicked himself loose from the earth," and particularly, "He was alone"—suggest that Kurtz cannot be taken simply as a symbol of transcendental evil; it is now clear that Kurtz's fate is of general interest because it is a consequence of his isolation, of his absolute freedom. He is a fully autonomous man, attempting to generate and enact his own moral truths, confronting the results of his freedom. In this passage we find the germinal "idea" of the story (to which Conrad had referred in his letter to Cunninghame Graham) most clearly embodied: that "safety" and "value" are illusions that can only be generated and preserved within a given society, while any attempt to place oneself outside these artificial, but necessary, moral structures will drive any *man* into a perilous condition of "excited imagination." The manager of the Central Station and the other "fools" of the story can never descend to the "heart of darkness" because they have no "imagination." What makes Kurtz remarkable is not only that he has lived in the darkness, but also chosen to leave it. *It* never leaves him, nor any man who has confronted it. We are never told the grounds on which Kurtz makes his final choice, and we may perhaps be left wondering why it is that Kurtz, who had been described as "hollow at the core," could suddenly become capable of his final, remarkable, victory.

It seems there are different kinds of hollowness, differently resonant. The manager and brickmaker are simply void; Kurtz's hollowness contains the nothingness of his universe. Like E. M. Forster's Marabar Caves, Kurtz echoes the final meaninglessness of all things.

That Kurtz's soul should become the theatre in which this "boum" echoes is not because he is immoral, but the reverse: he is the prototype of the idealistic man. His pamphlet (written for the International Society for the Suppression of Savage Customs) is charged with naive eloquence about the role of the white man in raising the natives to a "civilized" state, and presents what is at first glance an appealing moral position, faintly similar to Kipling:

> He began with the argument that we whites, from the
> point of development we had arrived at, "must necessarily

appear to them (savages) in the nature of supernatural beings—we approach them with the might as of a deity," and so on, and so on. "By the simple exercise of our will we can exert a power for good practically unbounded," etc., etc.

By taking advantage of conditions which allow him to assume the role of the benevolent deity, the white man can exercise his unlimited power towards good—or any other end that he chooses. Yet the assumption that a man in a state of absolute freedom will do good is nonsense; at the very "heart of darkness" every man desires, like Kurtz, to "take a high seat among the devils of the land." Hence we have Kurtz's final scrawl at the bottom of his pamphlet, "Exterminate all the brutes!" Kurtz's fate is that of any man who attempts to take upon himself the entire structure of morality.

The Nigger of the "Narcissus" refers to "the latent egoism of tenderness to suffering," a theme that is extended in *Heart of Darkness* to include the perception that altruism may ultimately be no more than egoistic self-glorification. A pitier always has a certain sense of superiority to the pitied, and this lurking wisp of self-congratulation seems inevitably to lead, in Conrad's vision, either to a feeling of self-pity or an assertion of the will to power. In *The Nigger of the "Narcissus,"* the men's pity for Jimmy and Donkin leads them to identify with the sufferings of the men whose cause they have taken up; in *Heart of Darkness,* Kurtz's assumption of the "white man's burden" is merely the pretext for an overwhelming desire for dominance.

When Kurtz dies on the steamer taking him down the Congo, his last words, "The horror! The horror!" impressive and even terrifying as they are, are nevertheless thoroughly ambiguous. They might represent Kurtz's final desire to return to the scene of those abominable satisfactions, be his judgment on the unworthiness of his end, a comment on the human condition, or a vision of eternal damnation. Marlow, however, is certain of his own interpretation; he sees Kurtz's last words as a confession, as a final attempt at self-purification: "a judgment upon the adventures of his soul upon this earth":

This is the reason why I affirm that Kurtz was a remarkable man. He had something to say. He said it. Since I had peeped over the edge myself, I understand better the meaning of his stare, that could not see the flame of the candle, but was wide enough to embrace the whole universe, piercing enough to penetrate all the hearts that beat in the darkness. He had summed up—he had judged. "The horror!"

At the "heart of darkness," it seems, there is a piercing clarity—a vision of man's fate so unendurable that it can only remain nameless:

He was a remarkable man. After all, this was the expression of some sort of belief; it had candour, it had conviction, it had a vibrating note of revolt in its whisper, it had the appalling face of a glimpsed truth—the strange commingling of desire and hate. . . . It is his extremity that I seem to have lived through. True, he had made that last stride, he had stepped over the edge, while I had been permitted to draw back my hesitating foot. And perhaps in this is the whole difference; perhaps all the wisdom, and all truth, and all sincerity, are just compressed into that inappreciable moment of time in which we step over the threshold of the invisible. Perhaps! I like to think my summing-up would not have been a word of careless contempt. Better his cry—much better. It was an affirmation, a moral victory paid for by innumerable defeats, by abominable terrors, by abominable satisfactions. But it was a victory! That is why I have remained loyal to Kurtz to the last.

Kurtz's final vision, then, is one both of the human predicament and of his own experience—is both general and particular, as J. I. M. Stewart points out:

Kurtz's evil courses—and this is the final terror of the fable—have brought him to the heart of an impenetrable darkness in which it is yet possible to *see* more than can be seen in daylight by those to whom no such journey had befallen. Kurtz's last words are a statement of the widest generality. They define one tenable view of man's situation in an alien universe. Alternatively, they define the only sense of himself that man can bring back from a wholly inward journey: that into the immense darkness, the unmeaning anarchy, of his own psyche.

In the light of this interpretation of Kurtz's final words, then, it seems that we must go back and re-evaluate exactly what Marlow meant when he indicted Kurtz as "hollow at the core." If Kurtz's fate is, as it seems, of universal significance, then to what extent can his degradation be said to be due to his inner hollowness? Marlow's remark that Kurtz's final words were an affirmation and a victory seems to contradict an earlier assertion that Kurtz was "hollow at the core." We appear to have two conflicting strands operating in *Heart of Darkness:* one which makes a distinction between those men who are "hollow" and those who have "inborn strength," while the other seems to regard Kurtz as a remarkable man who has made a journey into the self which few men could have endured. We may perhaps be left with the thought that the judgments that one makes about autonomous individuals are very different from the judgments that one makes about individuals as they relate to some social organization. Kurtz's egoism may damn him, but he is a remarkable man. Again, we turn to Nietzsche for a key to the enigma of Kurtz:

> Something might be true although at the same time harmful and dangerous in the highest degree; indeed, it could pertain to the fundamental nature of existence that a complete knowledge of it would destroy one—so that the strength of a spirit could be measured by how much "truth" it could take, more clearly, to what degree it *needed* it attenuated, veiled, sweetened, blunted, and falsified.

Kurtz—like his successor, Martin Decoud of *Nostromo*—sees too much, too clearly, to live through the experience.

After Kurtz's death, Marlow spends a long period hovering between life and death, undergoing the spiritual agony of a man whose illusions have been painfully shattered by viewing (and vicariously participating in) Kurtz's tragedy. Upon his return to Brussels, Marlow feels a different person from the young man he had been some months before. An initiate into the deepest knowledge, he is contemptuous of the unthinking smugness of "civilized" man. There is one question left to be answered: given that Marlow has had a vision of the "truth," what is he to do with it?

The answer lies in the scene in which Marlow visits Kurtz's Intended, in which his obligation to his "choice of nightmares" is finally clarified. Conrad once said that his method aimed at using a final incident to clarify his themes. As an example he cited "the last pages of 'Heart of Darkness' where the interview of the man and the girl locks in—as it were—the whole 30000 [sic] words of narrative description into one suggestive view of a whole phase of life, and makes of that story something quite on another plane than an anecdote of a man who went mad in the Centre of Africa." As Marlow enters the house of Kurtz's fiancée, he feels as if the spectre of Kurtz and his savage followers enters with him, seeking admittance into the world of commonplace truths and assured safety: "It was a moment of triumph for the wilderness, an invading and vengeful rush which, it seemed to me, I would have to keep back alone for the salvation of another soul." As he listens to her eloquent descriptions of Kurtz's goodness and love, it becomes clear to Marlow that her capacity to believe in Kurtz, to cling to her false image of his worth, is the sustaining force of her existence. Pressed to confirm her glorification of Kurtz in his own words, Marlow is faced with a critical moral dilemma. He has previously given his opinion on the subject of lying in unequivocal terms: "You know I hate, detest, and can't bear a lie, not because I am straighter than the rest of us, but simply because it appals me. There is a taint of death, a flavour of mortality in lies—which is exactly what I hate and detest in the world—what I want to forget." If Marlow tells Kurtz's Intended the truth of his experience with Kurtz, her "mature capacity for fidelity, for belief, for suffering"—the "few simple notions" on which *society* is based—will collapse, and the darkness that Marlow is seeking to contain within himself will have triumphed. Thus when pressed to confirm the genius and benevolence of Kurtz, he responds in terms which, while not untrue, are ambiguous. He makes three specific comments on what the girl takes to be Kurtz's virtues: he tells her that "We shall always remember him"; that "his words will remain"; and that "his example, too" will remain. She takes these remarks as laudatory, but Marlow (and of course the reader) recognizes their ironic tone. At the very end of his visit, Marlow is forced into a position in which an absolute lie seems necessary. Seeking "something to live with," the grief-stricken girl pleads with Marlow to reveal Kurtz's last words; he responds "the last word he pronounced was—your name." She is sustained in her illusion, and will be able to carry on with life sustained by her own "life-lie." The darkness is exorcized with this lie.

If it is a lie. A final ironic possibility remains—Marlow's remark may be ambiguous in the same way as his previous assertions: the "horror" and the name of Kurtz's Intended may be identical. But she is never to know this, can never know it. And so *Heart of Darkness* ends with the suggestion that truth is unendurable in the context of everyday life, that what one needs in order to maintain an assurance of safety and comfort is some sustaining illusion to which one can be faithful. The story closes with the anonymous narrator—his voice recognizably muted and chastened—looking over the quiet reaches of the Thames, and assuring us that it, too, "seemed to lead into the heart of an immense darkness."

*H*eart of Darkness
and Nineteenth-Century Thought

Ian Watt

Conrad isn't a philosophical novelist in the way that George Eliot, Thomas Hardy or George Meredith are; we don't feel in the presence of logical arguments or moral lessons. But if Conrad doesn't present himself as a thinker, he strikes us as very thoughtful; the intimations of his fictional world steadily invite ethical and even metaphysical response.

The basic conflict in this fictional world arises from a double vision; Conrad wants both to endorse the standard Victorian moral positives, and to express his forebodings that the dominant intellectual directions of the nineteenth century were preparing disaster for the twentieth. This conflict between the endorsements and the forebodings is most comprehensively expressed in the tension between Marlow and Kurtz in Conrad's ideological *summa, Heart of Darkness.* It has gradually established itself for the twentieth century as the supremely modern work in the Conrad canon; and it appeared, very appropriately, in the last year of the nineteenth century, and in the thousandth number of that very representative organ of high Victorian culture, *Blackwood's Magazine.*

Scientifically, Conrad was fairly well informed and, unlike most of the other great modern writers, he neither doubted nor discounted the findings of natural science. His position about the ultimate human implications of these findings, however, was deeply skeptical, and in several ways. Like Matthew Arnold in his essay

From *Partisan Review* 45, no. 1 (1978). © 1978 by Ian Watt.

"Literature and Science," Conrad diagnosed a deep intellectual muddle behind contemporary attempts to force a marriage between science and culture; for his own part he contemptuously rejected "the tyranny of science and the cant of science," and concluded that "life and the arts follow dark courses and will not turn aside to the brilliant arc-lights of science."

Some negative inferences, however, had to be drawn from science as regards human life, and they led to radical conclusions that brought Conrad fairly close to an existentialist position: the individual consciousness was destined to be in total contradiction to its physical and moral environment. "What makes men tragic," Conrad wrote to Cunninghame Graham, "is not that they are victims of nature, it is that they are conscious of it. . . . There is no morality, no knowledge, and no hope; there is only the consciousness of ourselves which drives us about a world that whether seen in a convex or a concave mirror is always but a vain and fleeting appearance."

It was primarily the two forms of natural science which most affected the general Victorian outlook—physics and biology—that had been decisive in making man see himself as the victim of nature. The traditional belief that the creation of the world, and of man, was a unique manifestation of God's providence had been fatally undermined long before by astronomy. Then in the nineteenth century geology had suggested, not only that the earth itself was a transitory phenomenon, but that, as Tennyson put it in *In Memoriam,* even man himself might one day, like the fossils in the books, become extinct and "Be blown about the desert dust, or sealed within the iron hills." Finally Victorian physics had confirmed this vista of coming extinction. For, it now appeared, our terrestrial planet had originated, not out of the hand of God but accidentally out of the cooling gases of the sun; and the formulation of the second law of thermodynamics by Lord Kelvin in 1851 seemed to mean that the destiny of the earth was to end in cold and drought through the diffusion of heat-energy.

This astrophysical pessimism, widely popularized by Balfour Stewart's *The Conservation of Energy* in 1873, soon became a standard feature of late Victorian thought. As Edward Carpenter wrote about the universe of his youth: "one of its properties was that it could run down like a clock, and would eventuate in time in a cold sun and a dead earth—and there was an end of it." The eighteenth century had inferred a divine watch-maker from the operations of the celestial machine; it was now discovered that there was no watch-maker and that the watch's spring was running down.

This dispiriting historical perspective pervades *Heart of Darkness*. Marlow's first remark, as the sun sets over London, is "And this also . . . has been one of the dark places of the earth." Dismissing from our minds both the present lights on the shore and the glories of the national past enacted along the estuary of the Thames, Marlow harks back to the darkness which had here confronted the first Roman settlers in Britain; and we are made to see civilization, not as a stable human achievement, but as a brief interruption of the normal rule of darkness; the extent and duration of civilized order are as limited and brief as "a flash of lightning in the clouds," and, Marlow reflects, "We live in the flicker."

Like atomic physics in our day, however, it was biology which had the most important moral and political implications for the later nineteenth century. That some of these implications found their way into *Heart of Darkness* is not surprising, for Conrad grew up in the heyday of evolutionary theory, and Alfred Wallace was one of his favorite authors.

The main plot of *Heart of Darkness* is provided, in effect, by that aspect of the evolutionary process to which Marlow is exposed in his voyage further up-river. Marlow stumbles onto a grim historical variant of the law that ontogeny recapitulates phylogeny; the case of Kurtz demonstrates the process in reverse. His atavistic regression is brought on by the wilderness which, Marlow says, "whispered to him things about himself which he did not know, things of which he had no conception till he took counsel with this great solitude." At home everything conspired to keep Kurtz in ignorance of his true self; the police stopped him from devouring others or being devoured; but in the solitude his "forgotten and brutal instincts" revealed themselves as potent forces in his biological inheritance, and therefore as powerful arguments against the widespread distortion of evolutionary theory to support the Victorian faith in economic, social, political and national progress, the faith which originally animated Kurtz.

The strongest single support for the Victorian faith in progress was economic expansion, to which both Bentham and natural science had lent a theoretical rationale and an immense public prestige. Conrad, however, rejected the material and quantitative values of a commercial and industrial society: he saw only danger in "the blind trust in mere material and appliances"; he warned against "carrying humility towards that universal provider, Science, too far," and he viewed the Victorian hope that progress would automatically result from "the peaceful nature of industrial and commercial competition" as an "incredible infatuation."

Kurtz, of course, stands not only for the civilizing beneficence of economic progress, but for the other more spiritual components of the Victorian religion of progress. Evolution had replaced the traditional view of man's supremacy in the Divine plan with the idea that an equivalently splendid status could be attained through the working out of humanity's secular destiny. In Arthur Lovejoy's phrase, the "temporalisation of the Chain of Being" had substituted the law of historical progress for the lost belief in the perfection of God's providential design.

During the eighties and nineties the main ideologies that supported this kind of belief were social Darwinism and imperialism, whose doctrines were closely related. Social Darwinism, of which the most famous exponent was Herbert Spencer, supported the competitive economic order at home, and utilitarian theory in general, on the grounds that—to use his phrase in *First Principles* (1862)—the "survival of the fittest" was a law of nature, and led to human progress.

The same kind of thinking provided an ideology for colonial expansion. Merely by occupying or controlling most of the globe, it was assumed, the European nations had demonstrated that they were the fittest to survive; and the accelerating exportation of their various economic, political and religious institutions was therefore a necessary evolutionary step towards a higher form of human organization in the rest of the world. It was also widely thought—by Spencer, for example—that the dominance of the white races was itself the result of biological superiority, and this racial doctrine became particularly useful in enlisting popular political support for the imperialist adventures of the end of the nineteenth century. As Victor Kiernan has written, the "mystique of race was Democracy's vulgarization of an older mystique of class."

Conrad's own attitude to colonialism was complicated; but he had been lucky, from a literary point of view, in finding an ideologically perfect and patriotically unembarrassing example of the discrepancies between colonial pretence and reality. It was a pure case: first, because the Congo Free State was in theory international, and thus did not raise the question of national loyalty; second, because unlike most other colonies the Congo Free State was a conscious political creation; and third, because the whole world had listened to

public professions of exalted educational, moral and religious purposes from its founders, and then been forced to discover that these
verbal pretences masked what Conrad later described as "the vilest
scramble for loot that ever disfigured the history of human conscience and geographical exploration."

During the two decades between Conrad's arrival in England in
1878 and the writing of *Heart of Darkness,* many leaders of thought
were becoming convinced that the Victorian world order was col-
lapsing. *Heart of Darkness* is an expression of that conviction; and
its widely-shared rejection of earlier optimistic assumptions about
progress is clearly echoed both in the literature and the evolutionary
theory of the period.

A great many novels of the nineties have a note of apocalyptic
gloom. Grant Allen's 1895 novel, *The British Barbarians,* for instance,
pictured the twenty-fifth century as a relapse into anthropoid ani-
mality; and there is a sense of the impending collapse of western
civilization both in Nietzsche's *Twilight of the Idols* (1889) and in Max
Nordau's *Degeneration,* which was immensely successful in its 1895
English translation. The idea gained even wider currency from Os-
car Wilde's *The Picture of Dorian Gray* (1891), where Lord Henry
murmurs "*Fin de Siècle*" and his hostess knowingly answers "*Fin du
globe.*"

The most immediate basis for this loss of confidence in the future was probably political, but the implications of natural science
were also important.

Darwin himself had been in the main dubious about whether
any political or psychological deductions about man and his future
could be drawn from evolutionary theory; a good many of Darwin's
followers, however, had drawn such deductions, and, in the case of
the most eminent of them, Thomas Huxley, they had become increasingly pessimistic. In his influential and widely reported 1893
Romanes lecture on "Evolution and Ethics," a lecture which had the
optimism of Spencer as its main target, Huxley asserted an intrac-
table dualism between nature and human values which is in many
ways parallel to that which Conrad presented in *Heart of Darkness.*

Spencer had been sure that what he regarded as the necessary
law of progress meant that "evil and immorality" would disappear,
and "man become perfect." Huxley had no such illusions. He conceded that "after the manner of successful persons, civilized man
would gladly kick down the ladder by which he has climbed. He

would be only too pleased to see 'the ape and tiger die.' But they decline to suit his convenience, and the unwelcome intrusion of these boon companions of his hot youth into the ranged existence of civil life adds pains and griefs, innumerable and immeasurably great, to those which the cosmic process brings on the mere animal." The prospect of happiness or perfection, then, is "as misleading an illusion as ever was dangled before the eyes of poor humanity"; man will always "bring with him the instinct of unlimited self-assertion," so that his future will be "a constant struggle . . . in opposition to the State of Nature"; and this unhappy conflict will continue until "the evolution of our globe shall have entered so far upon its downward course that the cosmic process resumes its sway; and, once more, the State of Nature prevails over the surface of our planet."

Five years later, in 1898, even the sanguine positivism of Herbert Spencer had apparently evaporated and he was inclined to agree, writing in a letter to Grant Allen: "We are in the course of rebarbarisation."

Heart of Darkness, then, expresses a perspective that was very representative of many currents of thought in late nineteenth-century England; but it is representative in a very tangential way. Conrad's imaginative world seems wholly independent; the ideas don't stick out, or ask for support or confirmation. Thus the closeness of Conrad's moral and social assumptions to Huxley's later evolutionary thought is very striking if we compare Conrad's picture of man and society with that of Hardy, Wells, or Shaw; but we could hardly say that *Heart of Darkness* is about evolution; and even if one said it is about colonialism, or about the implications of colonialism for the colonizers and their civilization, the description would still seem both too analytic and too restrictive.

Yet in his own way Conrad was an intellectual, and his first mention of writing *Heart of Darkness* presented it in specifically intellectual terms: "The *idea* in it," he explained to his publisher, William Blackwood, "is not as obvious as in 'Youth'—or at least not so obviously presented," and added: "The subject is of our time distinctly—though not topically treated."

This description, written on December 31, 1898, when the story was barely begun, refers only to its most obvious ideological content: that is, as Conrad rather defensively put it in the same letter, "the justifiable idea" of exposing "the criminality of inefficiency and pure selfishness when tackling the civilizing work in Africa." This anticolonial tenor is very similar to that of Conrad's earlier story, "An Outpost of Progress," which had led Cunninghame Graham, an avowed Marxist who shared platforms with such men as Engels and Kropotkin, to write a letter of enthusiastic praise. What Cunninghame Graham had correctly recognized was a general political perspective very similar to his own definition of "the Imperial Mission" as "the Stock Exchange Militant"; and Cunninghame Graham was equally enthusiastic about the anticolonial first part of *Heart of Darkness*. Conrad, however, urged him to delay final judgment, writing that "There are two more instalments in which the idea is so wrapped up in secondary notions that You—even You!—may miss it."

Conrad nowhere specifies what these "secondary notions" were; but he gives a clue in a later letter to Blackwood when he says that the final scene, where Marlow finds himself forced to lie about Kurtz's end to the Intended, "locks in" the whole narrative "into one suggestive view of a whole phase of life."

One of the secondary themes "locked in" to the conclusion is presumably Marlow's view of women. At the very beginning of the story Marlow was quite unable to convince his "excellent aunt" who got him a job with the Trading Company that it was run for profit; and this led him to interject: "It's queer how out of touch with truth women are. They live in a world of their own." Marlow makes a similar comment when he first mentions the Intended: "Oh, she is out of it—completely. They—the women I mean—are out of it—should be out of it. We must help them to stay in that beautiful world of their own, lest ours gets worse." In the manuscript Conrad made this passage even more explicit, and anticipates Marlow's final lie to the Intended about Kurtz's actual end, by adding: "That's a monster-truth with many maws to whom we've got to throw every year—or every day—no matter—no sacrifice is too great—a ransom of pretty, shining lies."

Marlow's misogyny may seem a somewhat less disabling prejudice if it is set in the context of his general view of life. What he says clearly refers, not to the women who work in the office of the Trading Company, for instance, or to Kurtz's native mistress, but quite specifically to women of the well-to-do and leisured class to whom his aunt and the Intended, and presumably the womenfolk of his audience, belong. Marlow's perspective, in fact, assumes the Victorian relegation of leisure-class women to a pedestal of philanthropic idealism high above the economic and sexual facts of life. Since Marlow believes that it is only through work—more generally through a direct personal striving to master some external and objective force—that anyone can find "his own reality," it follows that the practical truths of life are not transferable from one individual to another, whether verbally or otherwise; and it further follows that, merely by allotting its women a leisure role, bourgeois society has in effect excluded them from discovering reality. It is by no choice or fault of hers, therefore, that the Intended inhabits an unreal world; but because she does, Marlow at the end finds himself forced to lie to her about Kurtz. One reason is that if he told the truth she would not have the necessary grounds in her own experience to be able to understand it; another is that since for all his seeking Marlow himself has found no faith which will move mountains, his nostalgia inclines him to cherish the faith that ignores them.

Work versus words is an even commoner opposition in Conrad than in life; and in *Heart of Darkness* the cognitive role of work is often made the dialectical opposite of another secondary theme—the self-deluding tendency of verbal communication. Kurtz is the most obvious example; he is, Marlow discovers, "very little more than a voice," a hollow soundbox of egotistic pretensions; and Marlow's "memory of that time" lingers round him still "like a dying vibration of one immense jabber." For Marlow, women such as his aunt and the Intended are destined to be the mere echo chambers of this jabber. His aunt's illusions about the civilizing work in Africa came to her only because she lived "right in the rush of all that humbug" which had been "let loose in print and talk just about that time," while the illusions of the Intended are only "the echo of [Kurtz's] magnificent eloquence." Both Marlow's aunt and the Intended unconsciously function as the facade for the operations of the manager and his cronies; they are indeed, as Kurtz's oil painting suggests, the blind publicists for the venal hypocrisies of the sepulchral city; and words are its whitewash.

Marlow sees both the Intended and Kurtz as pitiful victims of the unreal aspirations of their century. The developing imperatives of Romantic individualism had set up the ideal of absolute liberation from religious, social and ethical norms; and this trend was later reinforced by many others—most obviously by the utilitarian view of society as composed of an aggregate of economic individuals, by the democratic egalitarianism of liberal political theory and by the thought of Herbert Spencer, who assumed that the progressive differentiation of individuals was the ultimate and sufficient aim of the evolutionary process. All these views at least agreed that progress required the removal of most established economic, political and social "restraints"; and the harlequin's surrender to Kurtz thus represents his century's innocent but fateful surrender to that total Faustian unrestraint which believes that anything is justified if it "enlarges the mind."

Conrad's critical intelligence had arrived, independently perhaps, but supported, surely, by his quick sensitiveness to what he could use in the thought and speech of others, at an unformulated but resolute intellectual conviction which had much in common with that general tendency among so many of the thinkers of the later nineteenth century, who began from the assumption that reason was not the controlling factor in human affairs. This view, in very varied forms, controls the philosophy of von Hartmann, Vaihinger and Nietzsche, the psychology of William James, Bergson and Freud, the anthropology of Sir James Frazer and the sociology of Tönnies, Sorel, Pareto, Max Weber and Durkheim; all of these shared Conrad's total skepticism about progress.

As a naturalized Englishman and a sea captain, however, Conrad had also come to adopt other much more positive and conservative loyalties which supply some of the other secondary notions by which Marlow judges his experience in *Heart of Darkness*. Ford Madox Ford wrote that Conrad ideally "desired to be . . . a member of the ruling classes of England" in the stable days of Lord Palmerston, and the positive standards in *Heart of Darkness* have something of this early Victorian quality. These standards—roughly, Duty, Restraint and Work—are those by which Marlow lives; and in various guises they were a firm, indeed a notorious, presence in early Victorian thought.

John Stuart Mill wrote in his "The Utility of Religion" that it was characteristic of "an age of weak beliefs" that "such beliefs as men have" should be "much more determined by their wish to believe than by any mental appreciation of evidence." We can see this wish to believe both in Marlow and in Conrad. Thus in his first letter to Cunninghame Graham, Conrad wrote: "It is impossible to know anything," but added, "tho' it is possible to believe a thing or two." Marlow makes the distinction even more explicit in *Lord Jim* when he comments, "Hang ideas! They are tramps, vagabonds, knocking

at the back-door of your mind, each . . . carrying away some crumb
of that belief in a few simple notions you must cling to if you want
to live decently and would like to die easy."

One of the few stable points of reference in *Heart of Darkness,*
which Marlow much admires in others and what keeps him more or
less sane himself, is efficiency at work. This emphasis on the psychologically stabilizing function of labor is close to Carlyle's remark in
Sartor Resartus (1834) on "the folly of that impossible precept, 'Know
thyself,' till it be translated into this partially possible one, 'Know
what thou canst work at.'"

In Conrad's own day the idea of the supreme value of work had
been made the basic social and political issue not only by Marx, but
by Ruskin and Morris; while notions of group duty and discipline, a
necessary component of the imperialist mission as well as of the
nautical order, were advocated by W. E. Henley and Kipling. At the
back of these insistences was the Victorian nightmare that the disap-
pearance of God would destroy all social and moral sanctions for
individual conduct, and that thereafter, in Tennyson's words, men
would merely "submit all things to desire." The question, in its sim-
plest terms, was whether in a secularized world there would remain
anything which corresponded to the word "conscience." *Heart of
Darkness* continues this Victorian preoccupation. For instance, when
the dying Kurtz is said to have "judged" his life, Marlow is surely
implying the real existence of the conscience, of some inner moral
constraint.

Marlow's overriding moral commitment to civilization, however deluded, weak and unjust it is found to be, is rather similar to
that of Conrad's contemporary, Freud. Freud's observations had
forced him to a position which dramatically undermined the accepted psychological foundations of the social and moral order, since
man was shown to be unconsciously dominated, not by reason or
benevolence or duty, but by the omnivorous and ultimately unap-
peasable appetites of the id; and so, in *Civilization and Its Discontents*
and *The Future of an Illusion* Freud wondered whether any secular
mechanism could ever replace religion in controlling the aggressive
drives which led to war and hatred of civilization. Freud had a deeper
belief in systematic thought than Conrad, and Conrad was not inter-
ested in Freud; nevertheless, they shared not only the same dark view
of man's innate constitution, and the same conviction that culture
was based on repression of restraint, but a similar sense that the de-

structive tendencies of man which their vision emphasized must be controlled as far as possible, partly by promoting a greater understanding of the inherent darkness of the self, and partly by supporting the modest countertruths on which civilization depends. As against the more absolute negations of Rimbaud or Nietzsche, or the equally absolute transcendental affirmations of Dostoyevski or Yeats, both Freud and Conrad defend a practical social ethic based on their fairly similar reformulations of the Victorian trinity of work, duty and restraint.

The general modern tendency has been to overlook this aspect of the thought of Conrad and Freud in favour of its more dramatic and original destructive side; in effect both of them have been either attacked or praised more for what they saw than for what they said about it. In the process their insistence on the need to control the unconscious and egotistic sides of man has been misinterpreted or overlooked: and this bias has often been reflected in the modern critical treatment of Kurtz.

Kurtz dramatizes Conrad's fear of the ultimate directions of nineteenth-century thought. These directions are beautifully expressed in Auden's poem "In Father's Footsteps," which begins with a poignant valediction to the basic psychological strategy of the Victorian religion of progress as it assimilated the implications of biological evolution:

> Our hunting fathers told the story
> Of the sadness of the creatures
> Pitied the limits and the lack
> Set in their finished features;
> Saw in the lion's intolerant look
> Behind the enemy's dying glare,
> Love raging for the personal glory
> That reason's gift would add,
> The liberal appetite and power,
> The rightness of a God.

The "rightness of a God" was a role almost automatically conferred on the white European when he left home and went out to govern colonies. "All Europe," we are told, "had contributed to the making of Kurtz," and his motives, as well as his fate, are deeply representative. He goes out, first of all, to make money; he is thus a representative of economic individualism, a protagonist of the career open to talent in the free marketplace; and because he finds a more effective way of exploiting the ivory of the Congo he is naturally expected to become a power in the great Trading Company. Paradoxically, however, the Benthamite, utilitarian and imperialist modes of thought turn out to be not the historical contraries but the complements of Romantic individualism as it had been transformed into its later Bohemian, Decadent and Symbolist embodiments. Kurtz is a poet, a painter, above all a man with the power of words; and his final quest for absolute liberation from all the constraints of civilization makes him a symbolic parallel to the career of Arthur Rimbaud, who had turned his back on European civilization in 1875, and ended up as a trader and explorer in Abyssinia.

The representative importance of Kurtz's surrender to the drives of the unconditioned ego has been analyzed by Lionel Trilling in his essay "The Modern Element in Literature." Conrad's "strange and terrible message of ambivalence towards the life of civilization," Trilling writes, "continues the tradition of Blake and Nietzsche"; and Kurtz is a portent of the future, for "nothing is more characteristic of modern literature than its discovery and canonization of the primal, nonethical energies."

Kurtz, however, does not consciously seek to liberate these energies; he goes out as a member of the "gang of virtue," the benevolent liberal reformers who are going to bring the light of modern educational, political, moral and religious progress to the dark places of the earth. Unlike Rimbaud, or Gauguin later, Kurtz is an envoy of civilization, not a voluntary exile; he is "an emissary," as the brickmaker says, "of pity, and science, and progress, and devil knows what else." But in Africa Kurtz meets the ape and the tiger within himself, and eventually lets them loose. Given the opportunity, it appears, the autonomous individual will indeed "submit all things to desire," and far deeper than his social instinct, it appears, is the desire to do everything he wants to do and claim "the rightness of a God" for doing it.

This "rightness" finds a powerful sanction in Western industrial progress. Kurtz achieves supernatural ascendancy primarily through his monopoly of firearms; the idea is prefigured, ironically enough, in his report to the International Society for the Suppression of Savage Customs, where Kurtz begins from the premise that "we whites . . . must necessarily appear to them [savages] in the nature of supernatural beings—we approach them with the might as of a deity."

The harlequin confirms this basis for Kurtz's power: "He came to them with thunder and lightning, you know—and they had never seen anything like it." So, Marlow tells us, Kurtz later presided "at certain midnight dances ending with unspeakable rites, which—as far as I reluctantly gathered from what I heard at various times—were offered up to him—do you understand?—to Mr. Kurtz himself."

Marlow is horrified, and so, just before his end, is Kurtz, to understand what happens to a man who discovers his existential freedom under circumstances which enable him to put into practice the ultimate direction of nineteenth-century thought: to bestow on the individual all those powers and freedoms which had formerly been reserved for God. Man's last evolutionary leap was to be up to the throne that he had emptied; up, and yet, at the same time, it seemed, far down, and far back.

Heart of Darkness embodies that view of human destiny which Sartre summed up in his definition of man as "the being whose plan it is to become God." Conrad enacted the unreal exorbitances of the plan in the fate of Kurtz; for himself he tentatively preferred the humbler and irresolute moral alternatives of Marlow. Conrad's vision had no use for Christianity, mainly on practical grounds: "Christianity," he wrote in 1916, "is the only religion which, with its impossible standards has brought an infinity of anguish to inumerable souls—on this earth." The cardinal lesson of experience is a full realization of our fragile, lonely and humble status in the natural order; and here any theoretical system, whether philosophical, scientific or religious, is likely to foster dangerous delusions of independence and omnipotence. Thus in "Youth" Marlow prefers Burnaby's *Ride to Khiva* to Carlyle's *Sartor Resartus,* the soldier to the philosopher, on the grounds that: "One was a man, and the other was either more—or less." So, against all the unreal psychological, social and religious hyperboles of his waning century, Conrad decisively rejected both the more and the less; and in *Heart of Darkness* affirmed the necessity, as Camus put it, "in order to be a man to refuse to be a God."

Freud, Conrad, and *Heart of Darkness*

John Tessitore

That *Heart of Darkness* operates on a highly symbolic level few readers will contest, and indeed most criticism approaches it this way. I
do not wish to debate the notions that the novel is a quest, journey
or descent to hell or any other worthwhile interpretation, but rather
to show what each of these approaches has in common: that in nearly
every instance they are dealing either directly or indirectly with some
"journey within," and I suggest that this journey is not merely one
of Marlow's self-discovery as is so often concluded, but the much
greater journey of all civilization from its present (western European) state of development back to its primitive origins. Although
the novel's concern with the nature of civilization has long been recognized, the approach to the novel has been, almost without excep-
tion, symbolic or allegorical. The evidence for this approach is enormous: the river, the darkness, the "pilgrims," the penetration. We
need not abandon this perspective when it obviously has so much to
offer. There is, however, another perspective that promises to contribute heavily to our understanding of Conrad's work. Ralph Maud,
in his "The Plain Tale of *Heart of Darkness*," side-steps the battle of
symbols and attempts to address the novel's issues by examining its
surface structure—its action, the "Plain Tale" of his title. He asks
why Kurtz turns around after travelling 300 miles down river; just
when and how Kurtz is reduced to savagery; and precisely what is
"the horror" he speaks of. While I dispute his conclusions I applaud
his method.

From *College Literature* 7, no. 1 (1980). © 1980 by West Chester University.

Although it depends heavily on symbolism, *Heart of Darkness* is more psychological than it is symbolistic. This is to say (using an extreme example), Conrad is here much closer to Henry James and Dostoyevski than to Hawthorne or, in keeping with the symbolist vogue of his time, Poe. The comparison might not be so extreme after all. Listen to the utterances of Dostoyevski's Underground Man.

> Now I ask you: what can be expected of man since he is a being endowed with such strange qualities? Shower upon him every earthly blessing, drown him in a sea of happiness, so that nothing but bubbles of bliss can be seen on the surface; give him economic prosperity such that he should have nothing else to do but sleep, eat cakes and busy himself with the continuation of his species, and even then out of sheer ingratitude, sheer spite, man would play you some nasty trick. He would even risk his cakes and would deliberately desire the most fatal rubbish, the most uneconomical absurdity, simply to introduce into all this positive good sense his fatal fantastic element. . . . And if he does not find means he will contrive destruction and chaos, will contrive sufferings of all sorts, only to gain his point! He will launch a curse upon the world as only man can curse (it is his privilege, the primary distinction between him and the other animals) it may be by his curse alone he will attain his object—that is, convince himself that he is a man and not a piano-key! If you say that all this, too, can be calculated and tabulated—chaos and darkness and curses, so that the mere possibility of calculating it all beforehand would stop it all, and reason would reassert itself—then man would purposely go mad in order to be rid of reason and gain his point! I believe in it, I answer for it, for the whole work of man really seems to consist in nothing but proving to himself every minute that he is a man and not a piano-key! It may be at the cost of his skin, it may be by cannibalism!

Like his Russian precursor, Conrad uses his work to examine civilization and it discontents, a phrase which I do not borrow casually from Freud, for some thirty years later Freud was to put into analytical prose the very issues which Conrad had explored in his little novel. The kinship between these two men, the English-speaking Russian Pole and the brilliant Austrian Jew, is enormous, as I intend to demonstrate. This is not to imply that either was familiar with the other man's work; indeed, evidence points to the contrary. (It is unlikely that Conrad encountered Freud's writing until well into the twentieth century while Freud may never have read Conrad at all.) Nevertheless, mutual recognition is totally unnecessary for an examination of this kind, for it is enough simply to observe that two great minds found themselves arriving at identical conclusions and expressed those conclusions through the modes of their individual disciplines.

I

The smallest unit of society is the individual. What relationship, then, does the individual have to his society or, more basic still, how does he contribute to the formation of that society? This leads to yet further considerations: what must the individual lose or sacrifice in deference to the superstructure? are the vestiges of primitive selfhood truly eradicated or are they transformed, sublimated, repressed? why does the individual deliver himself up to society? and, lastly, how does the superstructure operate upon the individual to keep him safely in line?

The fundamental tension underlying man and civilization (in general) and Kurtz and *Heart of Darkness* (specifically) is the pleasure principle vs. the reality principle. The former, briefly stated, is based upon man's natural tendency toward pleasure. In early development this tendency is manifested in an instinct to separate the unpleasant from the ego and attribute it to some external object. In normal development the instinct is mitigated and controlled by experiential knowledge which teaches that some pain originates from within while, similarly, the source of pleasure is often not ego but object. The boundaries of the primitive pleasure principle are rectified and, says Freud, "In this way one makes the first step towards the introduction of the reality principle which is to dominate future development." (*Civilization and Its Discontents.* New York: Norton, 1961.) But let us consider for a moment what would happen if one did not take the first step toward the reality principle or, rather, took a step away from it.

Kurtz, we are told, is an extremely enlightened individual—a

poet, painter, essayist and humanitarian. The chief accountant calls
him "remarkable"; the station manager, "exceptional"; the brickmaker, "a prodigy." And the motley Russian, in a clumsy panegyric,
unreservedly adores him. He is, further, the quintessential Western
man: "His mother was half-English, his father half-French. All Europe contributed to the making of Kurtz." It was this man, Kurtz
the European, who first entered the Congo nine years prior to Marlow's journey; and it is during those nine mysterious, unaccounted
years that something happened. We know, too, through a marvelous
bit of dramatic irony that whatever happened occurred after the
composition of Kurtz's report for the International Society for the
Suppression of Savage Customs and before the addition of its hastily
appended postscript, "Exterminate all the brutes!" It requires little
imagination to realize that there is something basically incompatible
between the conventional trappings of European civilization and the
central Congo environment. As one firsthand observer noted at
the time—"after one has seen that even at the capital of Boma all the
conditions of slavery exist, one is assured that in the jungle, away
from the sight of men, all things are possible." The answer to just
why this is possible, as it comes from Freud, is the preservation of
primitive instincts.

> In the realm of the mind . . . what is primitive is so com-
> monly preserved alongside of the transformed version
> which has arisen from it that it is unnecessary to give in-
> stances as evidence. When this happens it is usually in con-
> sequence of a divergence in development: one portion (in
> the quantitative sense) of an attitude or instinctual impulse
> has remained unaltered, while another portion has under-
> gone further development.

The idea is frightening and yet it is one which we today regard almost as common knowledge. Still, simply acknowledging the existence of these instincts does not explain how Kurtz came to be controlled by them. We must seek the motive—what might even prove
to be the necessity—for their release.

"Life, as we find it, is too hard for us," says Freud; "it brings us
too many pains, disappointments and impossible tasks. In order to
bear it we cannot dispense with palliative measures." If, in speaking
of the average man, the observation seems valid, how much more so
it must be in the case of Kurtz. For Kurtz, Marlow tells his companions aboard the *Nellie,* was unable to marry his Intended due to in-

adequate means and therefore joined the Belgian company in search of his fortune. In a very real sense, Kurtz had been driven by necessity to the Congo and away from everything he held dear. Surely this illustrates an extreme instance of pain and disappointment, requiring the strongest dose of "palliative measures."

These measures are of three sorts: powerful deflections, substitutive satisfactions and intoxicating substances. Let us examine them individually.

Powerful deflections, says Freud, "cause us to make light of our misery." The chief single deflection for Kurtz was undoubtedly the all engrossing search for ivory, a job at which he proved an enormous success. Means, of course, eventually (again we can only approximate the moment, it being in the realm of the "unknowable") gave way to ends, and when Marlow asks the young Russian how Kurtz came to possess such enormous quantities of ivory when he had nothing to trade, the latter replies succinctly, "There's a good lot of cartridges left even yet."

Freud has noted that work, more than any other conduct of life, attaches the individual to reality.

> The possibility it offers of displacing a large amount of libidinal components, whether *narcissistic, aggressive or even erotic,* on to professional work and on to the human relations connected with it lend it a value by no means second to what it enjoys as something indispensible to the preservation and justification of existence in society [emphasis mine].

Here Conrad is unquestionably in agreement. The most obvious illustration is the chief accountant to whom Marlow amusingly refers as "this miracle." Literally surrounded by death and squalor, the chief accountant sits at his desk in a "high starched collar, white cuffs, a light alpaca jacket, snowy trousers, a clean necktie, and varnished boots." While the scene is obviously amusing, Marlow (and here one may infer Conrad) views it with unveiled admiration. "His appearance was certainly that of a hairdresser's dummy, but in the great demoralization of the land he kept up his appearance. That's backbone." Kurtz, on the other hand, represents a completely antithetical position. For him, work is not the means of sublimation but the very means by which he exercises his narcissism and aggression. (Kurtz's narcissism is so great it absolutely appalls Marlow: "'My ivory.' Oh yes, I heard him, 'My intended, my ivory, my station, my river, my—' everything belonged to him." As to his aggression, it hardly needs illustration here, but I shall speak of eroticism shortly.) What is the cause of this gross inversion? The explanation lies in Freud's qualification that to reap the benefits of work the individual must first be attached to reality; i.e., subscribe to the reality principle. Kurtz's relentless and brutal pursuit of ivory illustrates the exercise of primitive instincts, instincts which are deeply rooted in the pleasure principle. In this manner [says Freud] "the connection with reality it still further loosened; satisfaction is obtained from illusions, which are recognized as such without the discrepancy between them and reality being allowed to interfere with enjoyment."

"Substitutive satisfactions" diminish our misery. Kurtz's satisfactions are, it seems, many. Again, the foremost satisfaction is the success with which he carries on his business, a success which has led to speculation concerning his advancement. "Today he is chief of the best station," observes the brickmaker with envy; "next year he will be assistant manager, two years more and. . . ." In addition he has apparently carried on for some while with his painting, poetry and, to the Russian, lectures on an infinite variety of topics, including love. The idea of love suggests still another source of satisfaction, the almost unimaginable sexual satisfaction suggested by "a wild and gorgeous apparition of a woman."

> She walked with measured steps, draped in striped and fringed cloths, treading the earth proudly, with a slight jingle and flash of barbarous ornaments. She carried her head high; her hair was done in the shape of a helmet; she had brass leggings to the knees, brass wire gauntlets to the elbow, a crimson spot on her tawny cheek, innumerable necklaces of glass beads on her neck. . . . She was savage and superb, wild-eyed and magnificent; there was something ominous and stately in her deliberate progress. And in the hush that had fallen suddenly upon the whole sorrowful land, the immense wilderness, the colossal body of the fecund and mysterious life seemed to look at her, pensive, as though it had been looking at the image of its own tenebrous and passionate soul.

Savage, superb, magnificent—the passage is the most purely sensual, purely erotic of any by Conrad. She is the consummation of flesh and energy, the personification of Lust. And yet there is a shadow which clouds this gorgeous image, a kind of mystery which links the savage queen to the "ineffable darkness" and "unspeakable rites" into which Kurtz has descended, and this in turn associates her with the third palliative measure.

"Intoxicating substances" make us insensitive to pain and disappointment. Freud speaks specifically of alcohol and certain drugs, but he mentions at a later point in his text that "there must be substances in the chemistry of our own bodies which have similar effects, for we know at least one pathological state, mania, in which a situation similar to intoxication arises without the administration of any intoxicating drug. *Mania*—no other single word so adequately captures Kurtz's appetite for lust, power, adoration and, finally, veritable godhead among the savages; and underlying all his appetites lie the "unspeakable rites." Precisely what these rites consisted of we don't know, for again Conrad has seen fit—rather, has seen the necessity—to preserve their obscurity. As a result, our imagination is so affected that the reader conceives horrors which could not, I suspect, be as effectively rendered into direct prose. There is reason to believe, however, that Conrad is chiefly referring to cannibalism, a practice which fascinated and appalled him. Two years after the writing of *Heart of Darkness* he again introduced the subject in the short story "Falk." One biographer traces the author's fascination with the subject back to his childhood. Conrad himself tells, in *A Personal Record*, how his grandmother told him of his Great-Uncle Nicholas Babrowski, an officer in Napoleon's army, who had once killed and eaten a dog.

> When the child assured her that he could never have done such a thing, she replied, "Perhaps you don't know what it is to be hungry." This account is presented in a manner which pretends to lightness and jocularity, but which somehow is never achieved. "The childish horror of the deed clings absurdly to the grizzled man. I am perfectly helpless against it."

Marlow does not know precisely what these rites consisted of nor does he wish to be told. (Here Marlow clearly exhibits the ambivalent sensibilities of his creator.) "I don't want to know anything of the ceremonies used when approaching Mr. Kurtz," he shouts at the Russian. At the same time, however, he is more fascinated than shocked by the spiked heads surrounding Kurtz's hut. Speaking of them, he calmly diagnoses Kurtz's deficiency.

> They only showed that Mr. Kurtz lacked restraint in the gratification of his various lusts, that there was something wanting in him—some small matter which, when the pressing need arose, could not be found under his magnificent eloquence. Whether he knew of this deficiency himself I can't say. I think the knowledge came to him at last— only at the very last. But the wilderness had found him out early, and had taken on him a terrible vengeance for the fantastic invasion. I think it had whispered to him things about himself which he did not know, things of which he had no conception till he took counsel with this great solitude—and the whisper had proved irresistibly fascinating. It echoed loudly within him because he was hollow at the core.

What the wilderness whispered to Kurtz was the truth that civilized men "moored with two good addresses, like a hulk with two anchors" had long ago ceased to hear: that man's principal ambition is pleasure and, if left unrestrained, he will do anything to obtain it. Here we begin to see the horror. "They strive after happiness," says Freud; "they want to be happy and to remain so. This endeavour has two sides, a positive and a negative aim. It aims, on the one hand, at an absence of pain and unpleasure, and, on the other, at the experiencing of strong feelings of pleasure." Kurtz, denied the benefit of external safeguards provided by Western society and armed with the "thunder and lightning" of his weapons (with a strong emphasis on the sexual implications of his battle paraphernalia), plunges into the reckless pursuit of pleasure, unconscious of the internal havoc he unleashes upon himself.

> He had taken a high seat amongst the devils of the land— I mean literally. You can't understand. How could you?— with solid pavement under your feet, surrounded by kind neighbours ready to cheer you or to fall on you, stepping delicately between the butcher and the policeman, in the holy terror of scandal and gallows and lunatic asylums— how can you imagine what particular region of the first ages a man's untrammelled feet may take him into by the

way of solitude—utter solitude without policeman—by the way of silence—utter silence, where no warning voice of a kind neighbour can be heard whispering of public opinion? These little things make all the great difference. When they are done you must fall back upon your own innate strength, upon your own capacity for faithfulness.

The whispering of a kind neighbour was replaced by the whispering of the wilderness, but while the new voice was sultry and alluring, what it had to say was not comforting. For all its temptation and fascination, its message was that which men most fear to hear, that happiness and pleasure are not and cannot be for them. "There is no possibility at all of its being carried through," says Freud; "all the regulations of the universe run counter to it." This, too, is the horror. Kurtz is defeated before he begins; his pursuit is a vain one. Still, he can not abandon the quest, for the wilderness has claimed him and he has surrendered to it. Like the hermit, he breaks with the real world and consequently with its controlling reality principle and, huddled in the womb-like interior of the Congo, he retreats into the still deeper interior of the self, ecstatically embracing the pleasure principle. I do not wish to suggest that the decision is a simple one—quite the contrary. The stress and pull between pleasure and reality is a strong and tiring one. When we finally meet Kurtz for the first time, he is exhausted and on the very edge of death. "I could see the cage of his ribs all astir, the bones of his arm waving."

That we are never told the specific cause of Kurtz's condition not only allows but strongly suggests a symbolic reading, one whereby his physical emaciation can be seen as the visible manifestation of a spiritual and psychological struggle which has wholly consumed him. The incident which most precisely illustrates the intensity of this struggle is given to us by Marlow, who overhears a conversation between the station manager and his rapacious uncle. Kurtz, apparently intending to return to the Central Station and, perhaps, to Belgium, was leading a huge convoy of ivory down the river when, after having travelled 300 miles, he suddenly turned around and started back against the current in the company of four black paddlers. The station manager and his uncle "were at a loss for an adequate motive." Marlow, characteristically rooted in the work ethic, thought at the time, "Perhaps he was just simply a fine fellow who stuck to his work for its own sake." But this is not the case, nor is it, as Ralph Maud would have us believe, a question of ambition. Kurtz turns round because he has been called back, because the wilderness has once again whispered in his ear and thrilled him with its horrible fascination; and even as he battles *upstream against the current,* just so he battles with his soul which struggles to revile the darkness. It is at once an act of denouncement and surrender: a denouncement of the reality principle and the civilization it sustains, and surrender to the anti-civilization which the pleasure principle offers in its stead. Yet the darkness is still further compounded for the choice is an artificial one—the alternative a sham. "But whoever, in desperate defiance, sets out upon this path to happiness will as a rule attain nothing. Reality is too strong for him. He becomes a madman, who for the most part finds no one to help him in carrying through his delusion" [says Freud]. By "delusion" Freud means the belief that one can successfully shut out reality, and reality here is the incontrovertible opposition of primitive (natural) instincts and the compelling social structures of modern (civilized) Western man. "The horror!"

II

The philosopher's vision of natural man has, over the ages, assumed a variety of forms, but generally speaking these forms can be categorized into two antithetical and irreconcilable visions of human nature: one which holds that man is innately good, the other that he is innately sinful. From Hobbes to the third earl of Shaftesbury, from Shaftesbury to Bernard Mandeville, from Mandeville to Francis Hutcheson—and so the debate rages on. The artist's vision has, predictably, followed a similar course. In *Robinson Crusoe* (1719) Defoe presents us with a man reduced to his natural primitive state. Alone on his island Crusoe must survive without the seemingly indispensable ornaments of eighteenth-century civilization; as Marlow phrases it, without the "butcher and the policeman" or "the kind neighbour ready to cheer you or to fall on you." That Crusoe does so with such extraordinary success (not merely surviving but thriving in a truly economic sense) clearly argues for a species that is instinctually civil and, armed with the barest tools and devices, will naturally strive to create a society in the enlightened Western tradition. This vision so delighted the great disciple of naturalism, Rousseau, that he referred to *Robinson Crusoe* as "a complete treatise on natural education" and one which, in the education of his imaginary pupil, Emile, "will, for a long time, consist of his whole library, and it will always hold a distinguished place among others." To the Hobbesian, this vision was grossly romantic; to the Freudian, aware of a factor unknown to his philosophic precursor, the "unconscious," it is painfully naive.

The argument against innocence is by no means a modern one. Indeed, one need only look to Genesis for a powerful refutation, wherein the rebellious angels could rebuke an order as perfect and divine as God's own. Through Milton we hear the voice of dissatisfaction rising ominously from the darkness: "Better to reign in Hell, than serve in Heav'n"; and now mingled with that voice is that of Kurtz: "he had taken a high seat amongst the devils of the land."

Freud, by way of definition, says, "'civilization' describes the whole sum of the achievements and regulations which distinguish our lives from those of our animal ancestors and which serve two purposes—namely, to protect men against nature and to adjust their mutual relations." Crusoe's history is, above all else, a documentation of "achievements" and "regulations" and hence a tribute to man's civil instincts. Society, Freud implies, is unified by common needs and common wants which are supplied primarily through scientific and secondly artistic triumphs. But what precisely is it that needs be regulated?

> Perhaps we may begin by explaining that the element of civilization enters on the scene with the first attempt to regulate these social relationships. If the attempt were not made, the relationships would be subject to the arbitrary will of the individual: that is to say, the physically stronger man would decide them in a sense of his own interests and instinctual impulses. Nothing would be changed in this if this stronger man should in his turn meet someone even stronger than he. Human life in common is only made possible when a majority comes together which is stronger than any separate individual and which remains united against all separate individuals. The power of this community is then set up as "right" in opposition to the power of the individual, which is condemned as "brute force." This replacement of the power of the individual by the power of community constitutes the decisive step of civilization.

Kurtz (and here his symbolic value is accentuated, the man who is "all Europe") enters an African society which recognizes the superiority of the community ("right") as exemplified in chieftain hierarchy, and destroys the essential structure of that society by transferring power to the individual, in this instance through guns ("brute force"). The antithesis of Crusoe, Kurtz is an anti-civilization figure. Left to rely upon his instincts and inner strength for nine years, Kurtz gradually weakens and eventually submits to an internal voice Freud calls "original personality, which is still untamed by civilization and may thus become the basis . . . of hostility to civilization." We may be shocked, even outraged, by Kurtz's behavior, but we should not be surprised. As both Frazer and Freud have made clear, in the primal family only the head of it enjoyed instinctual freedom while the rest lived in slavish suppression. The basic struggle of society, therefore, has been the wrenching of power away from the family's head and the distributing of it among its members (an action directly associated with the killing of the father, whether literal or symbolic). [According to Freud,]

> A good part of the struggles of mankind centre round the single task of finding an expedient accommodation—one, that is, that will bring happiness—between the claim of this individual and the cultural claims of the group; and one of the problems that touches the fate of humanity is whether such an accommodation can be reached by means of some particular form of civilization or whether this conflict is irreconcilable.

Irreconcilable—this is the ineffable darkness into which Kurtz has peered; knowledge of the unknowable, the numina, too great for mortals to withstand. This, of course, is the same darkness that Marlow, as if viewing its reflection in a glass, saw on the dying man's face. "Anything approaching the change that came over his features I have never seen before, and hope never to see again. Oh, I wasn't touched. I was fascinated. It was as though a veil had been rent." And so one had, for in gazing into Kurtz's face Marlow rent the veil of Moira. Kurtz has confronted the dark truth that the cultural claims of the group are irreconcilable with the individual's claim to freedom, and the vision grows still darker by the individual's willingness to put his desires before those of the community whenever it is physically possible to do so. Kurtz is *willing* to subjugate and exploit the tribes of the interior just as all Europe is willing to take part in the gruesome rape and slaughter of the entire Congo. At the moment of his death Kurtz confronts the most untenable reality of all—that the civilization to which he once subscribed, together with all its policemen and kind neighbors and public opinion, is itself an instrument of pure brute force.

> Did he live his life again in every detail of desire, temptation, and surrender during that supreme moment of complete knowledge? He cried in a whisper at some image, at some vision—he cried out twice, a cry that was no more than a breath:
> "The horror! The horror!"

He cried out twice. Perhaps once for himself, perhaps once for all the rest.

Some thirty-five years earlier Kurtz's Russian cousin, the Underground Man, faced the same reality and, as with Kurtz, it crippled him. In his blundering, naive, profound way, this sick, ineffectual civil servant shatters the stillness of the ineffable darkness:

> I will explain: the enjoyment was just from the too intense consciousness of one's own degradation; it was from feeling oneself that one had reached the last barrier, that it was horrible, but that it could not be otherwise; that there was no escape for you; that you never could become a different man; that even if time and faith were still left you to change into something different you would mostly likely not wish to change; or if you did wish to, even then you would do nothing; because perhaps in reality there was nothing for you to change into.

An Unreadable Report:
Conrad's *Heart of Darkness*

Peter Brooks

We need now to consider a number of issues we have raised [previously], concerning endings, authority, repetition, and the transaction of narratives, in the context of the "crisis" in the understanding of plots and plotting brought by the advent of Modernism. Joseph Conrad's *Heart of Darkness*—published in the last year of the nineteenth century—poses in an exemplary way central questions about the shape and epistemology of narrative. It displays an acute self-consciousness about the organizing features of traditional narrative, working with them still, but suspiciously, with constant reference to the inadequacy of the inherited orders of meaning. It suggests affinities to that preeminently nineteenth-century genre, the detective story, but a detective story gone modernist: a tale of inconclusive solutions to crimes of problematic status. In its representation of an effort to reach endings that would retrospectively illuminate beginnings and middles, it pursues a reflection on the formal limits of narrative, but within a frame of discourse that appears to subvert finalities of form. Most of all, it engages the very motive of narrative in its tale of a complexly motivated attempt to recover the story of another within one's own, and to retell both in a context that further complicates relations of actors, tellers, and listeners. Ultimately, all these questions, and everything one says about the tale, must be reconceived within the context of Marlow's act of narration aboard the

From *Reading for the Plot: Design and Intention in Narrative*. © 1984 by Peter Brooks. Vintage Books, 1984.

Nellie at the moment of the turning of the tide on the Thames, in the relation of this narrator to his narratees and the relation of the narrative situation to the stories enacted within it.

Heart of Darkness is again a framed tale, in which a first narrator introduces Marlow and has the last word after Marlow has fallen silent; and embedded within Marlow's tale is apparently another, Kurtz's, which never quite gets told—as perhaps Marlow's does not quite either, for the frame structure here is characterized by notable uncertainties. Referring again to Gérard Genette's tripartite distinction of narrative levels, it is evident that in *Heart of Darkness* everything must eventually be recovered on the plane of narrating, in the act of telling which itself attempts to recover the problematic relations of Marlow's narrative plot to his story, and of his plot and story to Kurtz's story, which in turn entertains doubtful relations with Kurtz's narrative plot and its narrating. Marlow's narrative plot will more and more as it proceeds take as its story what Marlow understands to be Kurtz's story. Yet Kurtz's story has other plots, ways in which he would like to have it told: for instance, in his *Report to the Society for the Suppression of Savage Customs* (a plot subverted by the scribbled and forgotten footnote "Exterminate all the brutes"); or else the manner in which posthumously he commands Marlow's "loyalty" in retelling it—as lie—to his Intended. Ultimately, we must ask what motivates Marlow's retellings—of his own and Kurtz's mortal adventures—in the gathering dust on the Thames estuary.

One way to begin to unpack the dense narrative layerings of *Heart of Darkness* may be through the various orders of signification and belief—ready-made life plots—that the text casts up along the way: orders that marshal reality and might explain it if only one could believe them, if only there did not always seem to be something subverting them. One such order, for instance, is the Company, its door flanked by the two knitters of black wool, one of whom—or is it by now a third, to complete the suggestion of the Parcae?—obtrudes herself upon Marlow's memory at the moment of maximum blackness "as a most improper person to be sitting at the other end of such an affair." In the knitted web—shroud, pall, or is it rather Ariadne's thread into a dark labyrinth?—the Company's design reaches to the depths of the dark continent. The Company as ordering is related to the "idea": "The conquest of the earth . . . is not a pretty thing when you look into it too much. What redeems it is the idea only." The "idea" is the fiction of the mission, which upon inspection is seen to cover up the most rapacious and vicious of imperialisms. Here surely is one relation of order as ready-made plot to story in *Heart of Darkness:* a relation of cover-up, concealment, lie. Yet one should note a certain admiration in Marlow for the idea in itself: a recognition of the necessity for plot, for signifying system, even in the absence of its correspondence to reality (which may, for instance, suggest a reason for his effacing Kurtz's scribbled footnote before passing on the *Report to the Society for the Suppression of Savage Customs* to the press). The juxtaposition of ready-made order to reality, and Marlow's capacity to see both the admirable and the absurd in such attempted applications of order, is well suggested by the Company's chief accountant in the lower station, in high starched collar and cuffs, "bent over his books . . . making perfectly correct entries of perfectly correct transactions; and fifty feet below I could see the still tree-tops of the grove of death." The building of the railroad, with its objectless blasting of a path to nowhere, would be another example; even more compelling is perhaps the picture of the French warship shelling an incomprehensible coast:

> Once, I remember, we came upon a man-of-war anchored off the coast. There wasn't even a shed there, and she was shelling the bush. It appears the French had one of their wars going on thereabouts. Her ensign dropped limp like a rag; the muzzles of the long six-inch guns stuck out all over the low hull; the greasy, slimy swell swung her up lazily and let her down, swaying her thin masts. In the empty immensity of earth, sky, and water, there she was, incomprehensible, firing into a continent. Pop, would go one of the six-inch guns; a small flame would dart and vanish, a little white smoke would disappear, a tiny projectile would give a feeble screech—and nothing happened. Nothing could happen. There was a touch of insanity in the proceeding, a sense of lugubrious drollery in the sight; and it was not dissipated by somebody on board assuring me earnestly there was a camp of natives—he called them enemies!—hidden out of sight somewhere.

The traditional ordering systems—war, camp, enemies—lead to the logical consequences—men-of-war, cannonades—which are wholly incongruous to the situation requiring mastery. There is an absurd disproportion between the ordering systems deployed and the triviality of their effect, as if someone had designed a machine to produce work far smaller than the energy put into it. And there are many other examples that conform to such laws of incongruous effect.

The question of orderings comes to be articulated within the very heart of darkness in an exchange between Marlow and the manager on the question of Kurtz's "method" in the acquisition of ivory, which, we have already learned from the Russian—Kurtz's admirer, and the chief teller of his tale—Kurtz mainly obtained by raiding the country. The manager's rhetoric is punctuated by Marlow's dissents:

> "I don't deny there is a remarkable quantity of ivory—mostly fossil. We must save it, at all events—but look how precarious the position is—and why? Because the method is unsound." "Do you," said I, look at the shore, "call it 'unsound method'?" "Without doubt," he exclaimed hotly. "Don't you?" . . . "No method at all," I murmured after a while. "Exactly," he exulted. "I anticipated this. Shows a complete want of judgment. It is my duty to point it out in the proper quarter." "Oh," said I, "that fellow—what's his name?—the brickmaker, will make a readable report for you." He appeared confounded for a moment. It seemed to me I had never breathed an atmosphere so vile, and I turned mentally to Kurtz for relief—positively for relief.

The result of this exchange is that Marlow finds himself classified with those of "unsound method," which, of course, is a way of moralizing as lapse from order any recognition of the absence of order, using the concept of disorder to conceal the radical condition of orderlessness. The manager's language—"unsound method," "want of judgment," "duty to point it out in the proper quarter"—refers to ordering systems and in so doing finds a way to mask perception of what Kurtz's experience really signifies. The "readable report," which Marlow notes to be the usual order for dealing with such deviations as Kurtz's, would represent the ultimate system of false ordering, ready-made discourse. What we really need, Marlow seems to suggest, is an *unreadable* report—something like Kurtz's *Report,* perhaps, with its utterly contradictory messages, or perhaps Marlow's eventual retelling of the whole affair.

The text, then, appears to speak of a repeated "trying out" of orders, all of which distort what they claim to organize, all of which may indeed cover up a very lack of possibility of order. This may suggest one relationship between story and narrative plot in the text: a relationship of disquieting uncertainty, where story never appears to be quite matched to the narrative plot that is responsible for it. Yet the orders tried out in *Heart of Darkness* may in their very tenuousness be necessary to the process of striving toward meaning: as if to say that the plotting of stories remains necessary even where we have ceased to believe in the plots we use. Certain minimum canons of readability remain necessary if we are to be able to discern the locus of the necessarily unreadable.

Marlow's own initial relationship to the matter of orderings is curious, and recognized by himself as such. Marlow is eminently the man of work, proud of his seamanship, concerned with what he calls the "surface-truth" of steering, mechanics, repairs, devoted to the values of the master mariner codified in Towson's (or Towser's) *An Inquiry into some Points of Seamanship:* "Not a very enthralling book; but at the first glance you could see there a singleness of intention, an honest concern for the right way of going to work, which made these pages . . . luminous with another than a professional light." Yet as he presents his decision to undertake his African journey, it appears capricious, irrational, unmotivated. The decision reaches back to his boyhood passion for maps—which are another external ordering of reality—yet particularly his attraction to the unmapped within them, to their blank spaces. The space to which he will journey in the story recounted in *Heart of Darkness*—for convenience, we may call it the Congo, though it is never so named, never named at all, in the text—appeared "the biggest, the most blank, so to speak." By the time of his journey, the blank has been filled in, "with rivers and lakes and names"; indeed, possibly it has been filled overfull with "ideas," for "It had become a place of blackness." But blackness appears to motivate as strongly as blankness. Marlow in fact appears to recognize that his explanation lacks coherence, when he goes on to describe the "mighty big river . . . resembling an immense snake uncoiled," and himself as the "silly little bird" that is "fascinated" by the snake—so fascinated that he began to have recourse, as he never had before, to women relatives on the continent, in order to have a captaincy in the Company trading on the river. The desire for the journey is childish, absolute, persistent through contradictions; the journey itself appears compulsive, gratuitous, unmotivated. In the manner of Marlow himself, the reader must, in the absence of clear purpose or goal to the journey, be content with a general "fascination." The point bears some insistence, for Marlow's description of his trip up the river will in fact be also a description of how the journey came to be motivated: of the precipitation of a motivating plot within the originally unmotivated journey, and narrative.

"Going up that river was like travelling back to the earliest beginnings of the world. . . ." The way up is the way back: Marlow's individual journey repeats, ontogenetically, a kind of reverse phylogeny, an unraveling of the threads of civilization. His quest, we might say, is also an inquest, an investigation leading toward beginnings and origins; and the traditional story line of the journey comes to be doubled by the more specifically goal-oriented plot line of the inquest. What makes it so is his discovery that he has been preceded in his journey by the "remarkable" Mr. Kurtz, who becomes the object of inquest, providing a motive for the previously gratuitous voyage. Kurtz in fact provides a magnetizing goal of quest and inquest since he not only has led the way up the river, he has also returned upriver instead of coming back to the Central Station as he was supposed to do: Marlow indeed is able to "see Kurtz for the first time," in his imagination, in this return upriver, "setting his face towards the depths of the wilderness." It can in fact be pieced together from various remarks of the Company officials that the very reason for Marlow's being sent on his journey upriver is to detect the meaning and the consequences of Kurtz's return upriver—a presiding intention to his voyage of which Marlow becomes aware only in its midst, at the Central Station. It is thus gradually impressed upon Marlow, and the reader, that Marlow is in a state of belatedness or secondariness in relation to the forerunner; his journey is a repetition, which gains its meaning from its attachment to the prior journey. Marlow's plot (*sjužet*) repeats Kurtz's story (*fabula*), takes this as its motivating force—and then will seek also to know and to incorporate Kurtz's own plot for his story.

So it is that Marlow's inquest, in the manner of the detective's, becomes the retracing of the track of a precursor. We noted earlier, in the discussion of Conan Doyle's "The Musgrave Ritual," that the detective story in its classic form is built on the overlay or superimposition of two temporal orders, the time of the crime (events and motives leading up to the crime) and the time of the inquest (events and motives leading away from the crime, but aimed at reconstructing it), the former sequence *in absentia,* lost to representation except insofar as it can be reconstructed in the time of the inquest, the latter *in praesentia* but existing merely to actualize the absent sequence of the crime. Tzvetan Todorov, we saw, identified the relation of these two orders as the relation of *fabula* to *sjužet* that one finds in any narrative: a story postulated as prior gone over by a narrative plot that claims thereby to realize it. The detective story may in this manner lay bare the structure of any narrative, particularly its claim to be a retracing of events that have already occurred. The detective retracing the trace of his predecessor and thus uncovering and constructing the meaning and the authority of the narrative represents the very process of narrative representation. This couple, the criminal precursor and the latecomer detective, has special relevance to the situation of Marlow and Kurtz. No more than the detective's, Marlow's narrative is not primary: it attaches itself to another's story, seeking there its authority; it retraces another's path, repeats a journey already undertaken.

In Marlow's narrative, then, we witness the formation of motivation in the middle of the journey, though in his act of narration this motivation may stand at its very inception, as part of the very motive of telling, since his own story has become narratable only in relation to Kurtz's. In a phrase that marks his first explicit recognition of a goal to his journey, and hence of a plot to his story, Marlow states, "Where the pilgrims imagined it [the steamboat] crawled to I don't know. To some place they expected to get something. I bet! For me it crawled toward Kurtz—exclusively." The reason for Marlow's choice of this "exclusive" and seemingly arbitrary motivation is made more specific following the attack on the steamboat, in a manner that helps us to understand the uses of plot. Thinking that the attack may betoken the death of Kurtz (later we learn that Kurtz himself ordered the attack), Marlow feels an "extreme disappointment," as if "I had travelled all this way for the sole purpose of talking with Mr. Kurtz. Talking with. . . ." His choice of terms to image his anticipated meeting with Kurtz now leads him to recognition that it was indeed Kurtz as talker that he sought:

> I . . . became aware that this was exactly what I had been looking forward to—a talk with Kurtz. I made the strange discovery that I had never imagined him as doing, you know, but as discoursing. . . . The man presented himself

> as a voice. . . . The point was in his being a gifted crea-
> ture, and that of all his gifts the one that stood out preëm-
> inently, that carried with it a sense of real presence, was
> his ability to talk, his words—the gift of expression, the
> bewildering, the illuminating, the most exalted and the
> most contemptible, the pulsating stream of light, or the
> deceitful flow from the heart of an impenetrable darkness.

The definition of Kurtz through his "gift of expression" and as "a voice," and Marlow's postulation of this definition of Kurtz as the motivating goal of his own journey, serve to conceptualize the narrative end as expression, voice, articulation, or what Walter Benjamin termed simply "wisdom": the goal of all storytelling which, with the decline of traditional oral transmission, has in the "privatized" genre of the novel come to be defined exclusively as the meaning of an individual life. And we have seen that in Benjamin's argument, the meaning of a life cannot be known until the moment of death: it is at death that a life first assumes transmissible form—becomes a completed and significant statement—so that it is death that provides the authority or "sanction" of narrative. The deathbed scene of the nineteenth-century novel eminently represents the moment of summing-up of a life's meaning and a transmission of accumulated wisdom to succeeding generations. Paternal figures within novels write their own obituaries, transmitting to the younger protagonists something of the authority necessary to view the meaning of their own lives retrospectively, in terms of the significance that will be brought by the as yet unwritten end.

To Marlow, Kurtz is doubly such a deathbed figure and writer of obituary. In the first place, he has reached his journey's end, he is lodged in the heart of darkness and it is from that "farthest point of navigation" that he offers his discourse, that "pulsating stream of light" or "deceitful flow." Kurtz has reached further, deeper than anyone else, and his gift for expression means that he should be able to give articulate shape to his terminus. "Kurtz discoursed. A voice! a voice!" Marlow will later report. But by that point Kurtz's report on the meaning of his navigation into the heart of the jungle will be compounded with his journey to his life's end, and his terminal report on his inner descent into darkness. So that Kurtz's discourse stands to make sense of Marlow's voyage and his life, his journey and his inquest: to offer that final articulation that will give a mean-

ing to journey and experience here at what Marlow has doubly identified as "the farthest point of navigation and the culminating point
of my experience." Kurtz is he who has already turned experience
into Benjamin's "wisdom," turned story into well-formed narrative
plot, matter into pure voice, and who stands ready to narrate life's
story in significant form. Marlow's own narrative can make sense
only when his inquest has reached a "solution" that is not a simple
detection but the finding of a message written at and by the death of
another. The meaning of his narrative plot has indeed come to depend on Kurtz's articulation of the meaning of *his* plot: Marlow's
structuring of his own *fabula* as *sjužet* has attached itself to Kurtz's
fabula, and can find its significant outcome only in finding Kurtz's
sjužet.

For Kurtz, in the heart of darkness and at life's end, has "stepped
over the edge" and has "summed up." Since it is a "summing up"
that Marlow has discovered to be what most he has been seeking—
that summary illumination that retrospectively makes sense of all
that has gone before—his insistence that Kurtz has summed up is
vitally important. At the end of the journey lies, not ivory, gold, or
a fountain of youth, but the capacity to turn experience into language: a voice. But here we are forced to give closer scrutiny to
Marlow's affirmations and their curious self-cancellations. Noting
that after Kurtz's death he almost died himself, Marlow continues in
reflection on ultimate articulations:

> I was within a hair's breadth of the last opportunity for
> pronouncement, and I found with humiliation that prob-
> ably I would have nothing to say. This is the reason why I
> affirm that Kurtz was a remarkable man. He had some-
> thing to say. He said it. Since I had peeped over the edge
> myself, I understand better the meaning of his stare, that
> could not see the flame of the candle, but was wide enough
> to embrace the whole universe, piercing enough to pene-
> trate all the hearts that beat in the darkness. He had
> summed up—he had judged. "The horror!" He was a re-
> markable man. After all, this was the expression of some
> sort of belief; it had candour, it had conviction, it had a
> vibrating note of revolt in its whisper, it had the appalling
> face of a glimpsed truth—the strange commingling of de-
> sire and hate. And it is not my own extremity I remember

best—a vision of grayness without form filled with physical pain, and a careless contempt for the evanescence of all
things—even of this pain itself. No! It is his extremity that
I seem to have lived through. True, he had made that last
stride, he had stepped over the edge, while I had been permitted to draw back my hesitating foot. And perhaps in
this is the whole difference; perhaps all the wisdom, and
all truth, and all sincerity, are just compressed into that
inappreciable moment of time in which we step over the
threshold of the invisible. Perhaps! I like to think my summing-up would not have been a word of careless contempt. Better his cry—much better. It was an affirmation,
a moral victory paid for by innumerable defeats, by abominable terrors, by abominable satisfactions. But it was a
victory! That is why I have remained loyal to Kurtz to the
last, and even beyond, when a long time after I heard once
more, not his own voice, but the echo of his magnificent
eloquence thrown to me from a soul as translucently pure
as a cliff of crystal.

The passage is one that epitomizes all our difficulties with Marlow
as narrator, for the resonance of its ethical pronouncements seems
somehow to get in the way of the designation of a starker and possibly contradictory truth: the moral rhetoric appears in some measure a cover-up. Marlow explicitly confirms Benjamin's argument
concerning storytelling and wisdom, and confirms his need for
Kurtz as the paternal figure whose final articulation transmits wisdom. Kurtz "had summed up." And this summary articulation,
which concerns not only Kurtz's individual experience but also penetrates "all the hearts that beat in the darkness," comes from "over
the edge," on the other side, *beyond* life, or more accurately, on the
threshold of the beyond, with one foot on either side; whereas Marlow has only "peeped" over the edge. In his hypothesis that "all the
wisdom, and all truth" are compressed into this moment of termination and threshold, Marlow evokes the tradition of the "pan-
oramic vision of the dying": as he says just before the passage I
quoted at length, "Did he [Kurtz] live his life again in every detail of
desire, temptation, and surrender during that supreme moment of
complete knowledge?" The supremacy of the moment should in-
form Kurtz's *ultima verba,* his summing-up: in his discourse is
wrought his "victory."

And yet, when after considering that "all the wisdom, and all truth" may lie compacted in that last moment, that "last opportunity for pronouncement," Marlow states: "I like to think my summing-up would not have been a word of careless contempt," he may subvert the rhetorical system of the passage quoted by inculcating a major doubt concerning the proper characterization of Kurtz's "word." The uncertainties of Marlow's argument here are suggested by other curiosities of diction and rhetoric. "Better his cry" is a curious comparative to use in regard to a word that Marlow claims was *not* spoken (the word of careless contempt). "But it was a victory" appears somewhat strange in that one doesn't ordinarily introduce a clause by a concessive when the previous clause is ostensibly making the same affirmation. Marlow's discourse seems to shape itself in opposition to the anticipated objections of an imagined interlocutor. By protesting too much, he builds those putative objections dialogically into his own discourse, making it (in Mikhaïl Bakhtin's terms) "double voiced." Double voicing indeed is suggested by the evocation of the "echo" of Kurtz's voice. This "echo of his magnificent eloquence" becomes the most highly problematic element of the passage when, later, we understand that the "soul as translucently pure as a cliff of crystal" is Kurtz's Intended, and that the "echo" which she hears is a pure fiction in blatant contradiction to that which Marlow hears in the same room with her: a lie which Marlow is obliged to confirm as conscious cover-up of the continuing reverberation of Kurtz's last words: "The horror! The horror!"

This is no doubt the point at issue: that Kurtz's final words answer so poorly to all of Marlow's insistence on summing-up as a moment of final articulation of wisdom, truth, and sincerity, as affirmation and as moral victory. Marlow affirms that it is Kurtz's ultimate capacity to judge, to use human language in its communicative and its normative dimensions to transmit an evaluation of his soul's adventures on this earth, that constitutes his victory: the victory of articulation itself. And yet, "The horror! The horror!" is more accurately characterized when Marlow calls it a "cry." It comes about as close as articulated speech can come to the primal cry, to a blurted emotional reaction of uncertain reference and context. To present "The horror!" as articulation of that wisdom lying in wait at the end of the tale, at journey's end and life's end, is to make a mockery of storytelling and ethics, or to gull one's listeners—as Marlow himself seems to realize when he finds that he cannot repeat Kurtz's last words to the Intended, but must rather cover them up by a conventional ending: "The last word he pronounced was—your name." The contrast of this fictive act of naming—"proper" naming—with Kurtz's actual cry may suggest how poorly Kurtz's summing-up fits Marlow's description of it. Indeed, his cry so resembles the "word of careless contempt" that when we find this phrase in Marlow's account, we tend to take it as applying to Kurtz's last utterance, only to find that it is given as the very contrary thereof. Something is amiss.

We can concede to Marlow his reading of the ethical signified of Kurtz's last words, his "judgment upon the adventures of his soul on this earth"—though we may find the reference of this signified somewhat ambiguous: is the horror within Kurtz or without? Is it experience or reaction to experience? But we have a problem conceiving the signifier as fulfilling the conditions of the wisdom-and-truth-articulating function of the end. More than a masterful, summary, victorious articulation, "The horror!" appears as minimal language, language on the verge of reversion to savagery, on the verge of a fall from language. That Kurtz's experience in the heart of darkness should represent and be represented by a fall from language does not surprise us: this belongs to the very logic of the heart of darkness, which is consistently characterized as "unspeakable." There are the "unspeakable rites" at which Kurtz presides, the "unspeakable secrets" of his "method," and, at the very heart of the darkness—at the moment when Marlow pursues Kurtz into the jungle at night, to struggle with his soul and carry him back to the steamer—we have only this characterization of the dark ceremony unfolding by the campfire: "It was very awful." Critics have most often been content to point to the moral signified of such phrases—or to criticize them, and Conrad, for a lack of referential and ethical specificity—but we should feel obliged to read them in their literal statement. What stands at the heart of darkness—at the journey's end and at the core of this tale—is unsayable, extralinguistic.

It cannot be otherwise, for the heart of darkness—and Kurtz himself in the heart—is beyond the system of human social structures which makes language possible and is itself made possible by language: which is unthinkable except through and as language, as that which demarcates culture from nature. The issue is most directly addressed by Marlow when he contrasts Kurtz's position within the unspeakable and unimaginable darkness to that of his solidly "moored" listeners aboard the *Nellie:*

> It was impossible—it was not good for one either—trying
> to imagine. He had taken a high seat amongst the devils of
> the land—I mean literally. You can't understand. How
> could you?—with solid pavement under your feet, sur-
> rounded by kind neighbours ready to cheer you or to fall
> on you, stepping delicately between the butcher and the
> policeman, in the holy terror of scandal and gallows and
> lunatic asylums—how can you imagine what particular re-
> gion of the first ages a man's untrammelled feet may take
> him into by the way of solitude—utter solitude without a
> policeman—by the way of silence—utter silence, where
> no warning voice of a kind neighbour can be heard whis-
> pering of public opinion? These little things make all the
> great difference.

Language is here presented, accurately enough, as a system of police.
Incorporate with the *polis,* language forms the basis of social organization (which itself functions as a language) as a system of difference, hence of distinction and restraint, which polices individuality
by making it part of a transindividual, intersubjective system: precisely what we call society. To policing is contrasted the utter silence
of utter solitude: the realm beyond interlocution, beyond dialogue,
hence beyond language. As Marlow puts it when he struggles to
return Kurtz from the jungle to the steamboat, "I had to deal with a
being to whom I could not appeal in the name of anything high or
low. . . . He had kicked himself loose of the earth."

If Kurtz's summing-up may represent ethically a return to the
earth and its names (though the ethical reference of his last pronouncement is at least ambiguous), as an act of language "The horror! The horror!" stands on the verge of non-language, of nonsense.
This is not to characterize "The horror!" as the Romantic ineffable:
if Marlow appears to affirm an ineffable behind Kurtz's words, his
whole narrative rather demonstrates the nothingness of that behind.
Marlow continually seems to promise a penetration into the heart of
darkness, along with a concurrent recognition that he is confined to
the "surface truth." There is no reconciliation of this standoff, but
there may be the suggestion that language, as interlocutionary and
thus as social system, simply can have no dealings with an ineffable.
For language, nothing will come of nothing.

Certainly the summing-up provided by Kurtz cannot represent

the kind of terminal wisdom that Marlow seeks, to make sense of both Kurtz's story and his own story and hence to bring his narrative to a coherent and significant end. Kurtz's final articulation should perhaps be typed as more than anything else anaphoric, pointing to the unsayable dumbness of the heart of darkness and to the impossible end of the perfect narrative plot. In this sense, Kurtz's narrative never fully exists, never fully gets itself told. And for the same reason, Marlow's narrative can never speak the end that it has sought so hard to find, and that it has postulated as the very premise and guarantee of its meaning. Marlow's search for meaning appears ever to be suspended, rather in the manner of his description of his encounter with death: "My destiny! Droll thing life is—that mysterious arrangement of merciless logic for a futile purpose. The most you can hope from it is some knowledge of yourself—that comes too late—a crop of unextinguishable regrets." The logic of life's plot is never vouchsafed knowledge of that end which might make its purpose significant. Such knowledge as there is always is caught in a process of suspension and deferral, so that it comes too late. Marlow as the belated follower of Kurtz the predecessor is too late, as, the tale implies, he who seeks to know the end, rather than simply live it, must always be. Ends are not—are no longer?—available.

The necessary syntactic incompletion of the life story is referred to by the Marlow who is one of the narrators of *Lord Jim,* a novel contemporaneous with *Heart of Darkness:*

> And besides, the last word is not said,—probably shall never be said. Are not our lives too short for that full utterance which through all our stammerings is of course our only and abiding intention? I have given up expecting those last words, whose ring, if they could only be pronounced, would shake both heaven and earth. There is never time to say our last word—the last word of our love, of our desire, faith, remorse, submission, revolt.

Marlow here defines the "intention" of life as "utterance," as the articulation of Benjamin's "wisdom," and as the completion of that fully predicated sentence which to Barthes constitutes the classical narrative. Does this Marlow give up the other Marlow's search for the "summing up," or does he rather reaffirm that since it is unknowable in one's own life it must be sought in the voice of another, as in Kurtz's? The word "stammerings" may imply that the search for

utterance will always encounter a crossing of voices, creating a dialogic discourse of more complex reference and truth than the
heaven-and-earth-shaking last word.

Returning to *Heart of Darkness,* we must ask what we are to
make of Marlow's puzzling continued affirmation of Kurtz's "victory," and his proclamation of continued "loyalty" to Kurtz because
of this victory. Is it that Marlow recognizes his own continuing need
for the terminal articulation by which everything else makes sense,
and thus in the face of all evidence to the contrary continues to affirm
the articulate significance of Kurtz's final cry? In order to make sense
of his own story, Marlow needs an ending "borrowed" from another's story. In the lack of finality of the promised end, Marlow must
continue to attach his story to Kurtz's, since to detach it would be to
admit that his narrative on board the *Nellie* is radically unmotivated,
arbitrary, perhaps meaningless. As he has conceded at the start of his
narrative, the story was "sombre" and "not very clear. And yet it
seemed to throw a kind of light." His loyalty to Kurtz is perhaps
ultimately the loyalty of *sjužet* to *fabula:* the loyalty of telling to told,
of detective to criminal, follower to forerunner, repetition to recollection. It is only through the postulation of a repetition that narrative plot gains motivation and the implication of meaning, as if, in
the absence of any definable meaning in either *fabula* or *sjužet,* it were
in the fact of repetition of one by the other that meaning could be
made to inhere.

Marlow's "loyalty" to Kurtz is overtly tested in the last episode
recounted in his narrative, the meeting with Kurtz's Intended. She
insists that there must be a traditional pattern of transmission from
person to person, from one story to another, from precursor to those
left behind: "'Something must remain. His words, at least, have not
died.' 'His words will remain,' I said." Since she believes that the
meaning of Kurtz's life story lies in the words he has left behind, the
Intended naturally demands to know Kurtz's last words, those
which, capping the utterance expressing his life, should fix him se-
mantically for posterity, endow his story with authority. If up to
now Marlow has insisted that Kurtz's last words constitute a victory,
here he discovers that as an official conclusion to Kurtz's story they
will not do. The Intended asks that he repeat Kurtz's last words:

I was on the point of crying at her, "Don't you hear them?"
The dusk was repeating them in a persistent whisper all

around us, in a whisper that seemed to swell menacingly like the first whisper of a rising wind. "The horror! The horror!"

"His last word—to live with," she insisted. "Don't you understand I loved him—I loved him—I loved him!"

I pulled myself together and spoke slowly.

"The last word he pronounced was—your name."

Marlow's retreat here into a conventional ending to Kurtz's story, his telling of a lie—and Marlow hates lies because they have "a flavour of mortality"—marks a decision that Kurtz's last words belong to the category of the unspeakable. Language as a system of social communication and transmission, as the medium of official biographies and readable reports, has no place for the unspeakable; it is used rather to cover up the unnamable, to reweave the seamless web of signification. The cover-up is accomplished by Marlow's substituting "your name"—the name of the Intended, which we are never in fact given—for the nameless, as if to say that any proper name can be used, according to the circumstance, to ward off the threat of a fall from language. This substitutability of names, of course, marks a notable alterability of stories: the narrative of Kurtz composed by Marlow for the Intended is different from that told to the other narratees, those on board the *Nellie*. The way stories are told, and what they mean, seems to depend as much on narratee and narrative situation as on narrator.

That Marlow's narration on board the *Nellie* concludes—or more accurately, breaks off—just after he has told of his lie to the Intended suggests the link between his lie and his narrative. Having once presented a lying version of Kurtz's story, he apparently needs to retell it, restituting its darkness this time, and in particular showing its place in Marlow's own story. Marlow's lie on behalf of Kurtz's official story, alluded to early in his narrative, prior to the account of his meeting with Kurtz, has been from the start implicitly the most powerful motive to Marlow's act of narration, which comes to break the silence of dusk on the Thames without explicit raison d'être. By its end, Marlow's narrative has revealed the central motive that compelled his act of narration. He is not simply a teller of tales, but a reteller. He must retell a story, that of Kurtz, mistold the first time. And in doing so, he must complicate it by telling how he came to know it, thus adding another layer of plot and eventually transforming the relation of telling to told, so that is is finally less Kurtz's story that he tells than his own story inhabited, as it were, by Kurtz's story. The question may then be whether Marlow can tell the story "right" the second time around: whether the story that needs telling can properly be told at all, since proper telling may imply a conventional semantics and syntax that are unfaithful to Marlow's experience of Kurtz's experience of the heart of darkness.

This brings us back to the final issue we need to address, that of Marlow as storyteller, retelling his story on the deck of the *Nellie* to a certain group of listeners. Marlow's tale is proffered at a moment of suspension: the moment of the turning of the tide, as the mariners wait for the outbound tide in the Thames estuary in order to begin a new voyage. By the time Marlow falls silent, they will have missed the "first of the ebb." Marlow's tale inserts itself, then, in a moment of indefinable suspension between the flood and the ebb of the tide, at a decisive turning point that passes undiscerned to those who depend on it. This suspended temporality finds a counterpart in the first narrator's description of Marlow's tales as reversals or negative images of those usually spoken by seamen, in that they do not frame their wisdom in the conventional manner:

> The yarns of seamen have a direct simplicity, the whole meaning of which lies within the shell of a cracked nut. But Marlow was not typical (if his propensity to spin yarns be excepted), and to him the meaning of an episode was not inside like a kernel but outside, enveloping the tale which brought it out only as a glow brings out a haze, in the likeness of one of these misty halos that sometimes are made visible by the spectral illumination of moonshine.

This way of characterizing Marlow's narratives first of all puts us on warning that the structure of "framed narration" used in *Heart of Darkness* will not in this instance give a neat pattern of nested boxes, bracketed core structures, nuts within shells. If we consider how each of the inner frames opens and closes, we realize that in a traditional patterning we should have a structure in which the first narrator presents Marlow as the second narrator, who presents Kurtz as the third narrator; then Kurtz would tell his tale to its end and fall silent; Marlow would then finish his own tale, framing Kurtz's; and the first narrator would reappear to close the outer frame. In fact, Kurtz never fulfills the promise of a coherent inner frame, a core structure, for although we are told repeatedly that "he discoursed," we get very little report of what he said. Kurtz never assumes the narration of his own story, which comes to us in a curiously lateral and indeed nonnarrated form, from the Russian: "this amazing tale that was not so much told as suggested to me in desolate exclamations, completed by shrugs, in interrupted phrases, in hints ending in deep sighs." And since Kurtz's story in its telling becomes bound up with Marlow's, it never is clearly demarcated from its frames. Then, at the close of Marlow's narration, where we might expect the first narrator to step in with a closing comment—a final "summing up"—we have an apparent avoidance of explicit reaction to Marlow's narrative. There is simply citation of the director's remark that they have missed the first of the ebb (ambiguous indication of either inattentiveness or else absorption, pensivity) and the first narrator's final descriptive sentence: "I raised my head. The offing was barred by a black bank of clouds, and the tranquil waterway leading to the uttermost ends of the earth flowed sombre under an overcast sky— seemed to lead into the heart of an immense darkness." Thus there is a generalization of the darkness at the heart of Marlow's (and Kurtz's) stories, rather than any defining illumination. The Thames, which initially was presented as leading up to a place of darkness—a place of gloom, and once itself a heart of darkness—now leads out to darkness as well. Darkness is everywhere visible. The encompassing darkness offers one realization of the image the first narrator has used to describe Marlow's tales, where meaning is not within but "enveloping." The tale, that image tells us, does not contain meaning, but rather brings it out as a surrounding medium, acting itself as a virtual source of illumination which must be perceived in that which, outside itself, it illuminates: "as a glow brings out a haze," in the manner of a misty halo made visible "by the spectral illumination of moonshine." Marlow's tale makes the darkness visible.

If we ask what a meaning that is outside rather than within the narrative might be, what status it might have, we are forced to the conclusion that such meaning must reside in the relation between the tale's telling and its listening, in its reception, its transaction, in the interlocutionary relation. The truth value of Marlow's narrative must be in what his listeners can do with it. Perhaps the most important dramatization of interlocution comes at the moment when Marlow appeals to his listeners to "see":

"He [Kurtz] was just a word to me. I did not see the man in the name any more than you do. Do you see him? Do you see the story? Do you see anything? It seems to me I am trying to tell you a dream—making a vain attempt, because no relation of a dream can convey the dream-sensation, that commingling of absurdity, surprise, and bewilderment in a tremor of struggling revolt, that notion of being captured by the incredible which is of the very essence of dreams. . . ."

He was silent for a while.

". . . No, it is impossible; it is impossible to convey the life-sensation of any given epoch of one's existence—that which makes its truth, its meaning—its subtle and pene-trating essence. It is impossible. We live, as we dream—alone. . . ."

He paused again as if reflecting, then added—

"Of course in this you fellows see more than I could then. You see me, whom you know. . . ."

It had become so pitch dark that we listeners could hardly see one another. For a long time already he, sitting apart, had been no more to us than a voice. There was not a word from anybody. The others might have been asleep, but I was awake. I listened, I listened on the watch for the sentence, for the word, that would give me the clue to the faint uneasiness inspired by this narrative that seemed to shape itself without human lips in the heavy night-air of the river.

Marlow's appeal to vision, and his attempt to make his own visual presence into his listeners' surrogate assurance of truth in Kurtz's story—the substitute for eyewitness experience—are, of course, subverted by the first narrator's comment that he and the other lis-teners could in fact no longer see Marlow (or even one another). Like Kurtz himself, Marlow has become a disembodied voice. If Marlow is simply voice, then the authority of his narrative depends wholly on his verbal act, on rhetoric. And as a listener to Marlow's rhetoric, the first narrator—Marlow's principal narratee—tells us that he is on the watch "for the sentence, for the word" that would solve the enigma and the mystery of Marlow's narrative. The first narrator thus characterizes himself as an obtuse narratee, for pinning down "the sentence" and "the word" is precisely what Marlow's narrative will not and cannot do—indeed, what Marlow's narratives never do, according to the first narrator's own characterization of them as "inconclusive." The nearest Marlow will come to speaking "the sentence," "the word," is his report of Kurtz's summing-up, a non-sentence and words that fail as definition, which necessitate the continuing effort to tell, where telling never coincides with designation but is rather a perpetual slippage of meaning, a movement forward in a metonymic chain which can never fix meaning—for meaning is not, whatever the Intended may think, a matter of nomenclature—but simply point to its place, contextualize the desire for it and the movement toward it.

The impossibility of summing-up, the impossibility of designating meaning as within the narrative frame, explains why Marlow must retell his tale on board the *Nellie,* seeking meaning in the "spectral illumination" of narrative transaction. If framed narration in general offers a way to make explicit and to dramatize the motive for storytelling, *Heart of Darkness* shows the motive for retelling. Repetition appears to be a product of failure in the original telling—Kurtz's failure to narrate his own story satisfactorily, Marlow's lying version of Kurtz's story to the Intended—just as, in Freud's terms, repetition and working through come into play when orderly memory of the past—recollection of it *as* past—is blocked. We are fully within the dynamics of the transference. But it does not seem possible to conclude that Marlow's retelling on the *Nellie* is wholly a success: it does not meet the standards of intelligibility sought by the first narrator, and the most that can be said of the other narratees is that they are possibly (though not certainly) absorbed by the tale. We have a feeling at the end of Marlow's act of narration that retelling of his tale will have to continue: that the ambiguous wisdom he has transmitted to his listeners will have to be retransmitted by them as narrative to future listeners. The process is potentially infinite, any closure or termination merely provisional. *Heart of Darkness* does not "end"; it is a potentially interminable analysis that simply breaks off.

Any future retelling of Marlow's tale of Kurtz's story will have to be narrative in nature because there is no way to state its kernel, its wisdom, directly: this can only be approached metonymically, through a trying-out of orders, through plottings. And these will never take you there, they will only indicate where "there" might be located. Meaning will never lie in the summing-up but only in transmission: in the passing-on of the "horror," the taint of knowledge gained. Meaning is hence dialogic in nature, located in the interstices of story and frame, born of the relationship between tellers and listeners. Meaning is indeed the implicit dialogue itself, the "set" of the teller's message toward his listener as much as toward the matter of his tale. Marlow is as fully concerned with the hearing as with the telling of his tale and its truth, equally concerned with the "phatic" as with the "emotive" and "referential" functions of language. If meaning must be conceived as dialogic, dialogue represents a centerless and reversible structure, engendering an interminable process of analysis and interpretation, a dynamics of the transference in which the reader is solicited not only to understand the story, but to complete it: to make it fuller, richer, more powerfully ordered, and therefore more hermeneutic. Summing-up and dialogue are offered as two different modes of understanding, each incompatible with the other, yet neither exclusive. Marlow needs the postulation of Kurtz's summing-up in order to make basic sense of his own narrative. Failing himself to sum up, he must pass on his implication as narratee of Kurtz's story to his listeners, implicating them in turn as narratees, trapping them in the dialogic relationship. Figured here as well is the reader's relationship to the text. The reader's own incapacity to sum up—the frustration promoted by the text—is consubstantial with his dialogic implication in the text. The reader is necessarily part of the process of transmission in this tale that is ultimately most of all about transmission.

I have argued that one finally needs to read *Heart of Darkness* as act of narration even more than as narrative or as story. It shows this act to be far from innocent, indeed as based perhaps most of all on the need and the desire to implicate one's listeners in a taint one can't live with alone. It is not simply, and not so much, that confessing excuses but that properly managed it taints. If the listener has listened, he has assumed the position of "thou" to an "I." Reassuming the first-person pronoun for himself, he makes the former "I" into a "thou." The intersubjective and reversible pattern of dialogue has been created. Why are you telling me this? the interlocutor may want to ask—but by the time he comes to make such a response, it is already too late: like the Ancient Mariner's Wedding Guest, he has been made to hear. If a number of nineteenth- and twentieth-century narrative texts present sophisticated versions of traditional oral storytelling, it is because this gives them a way to force the reader into transferential relationship with what he may not want to see or hear.

Yet another characteristic peculiar to late nineteenth- and early twentieth-century narrative—that which we characterize as modernist—appears to emerge from our study of *Heart of Darkness*. This is the implication that all stories are in a state of being retold, that there are no more primary narratives. Marlow must repeat Kurtz's story, and presumably his listeners will have to repeat Marlow's story of Kurtz's story. Indeed, the very start of Marlow's narrative suggests an infinite possibility of repetition when he reaches back nineteen hundred years to imagine the Roman commander navigating up the Thames, into a land of savagery: a further level of *fabula,* an ancient historical story that all the modern stories must rehearse. One could demonstrate in a number of texts—James's *The Aspern Papers,* for instance, or Gide's *Les Faux-Monnayeurs,* or Faulkner's *Absalom, Absalom!,* even Proust's *Recherche* insofar as Marcel repeats the story of Swann in love—that there seems to be a need for protagonists and storytellers, and particularly protagonists *as* storytellers, to attach their narratives to someone else's, to be ever the belated followers of the track of another. Do we find here once again the influence of the detective story, that genre invented by the nineteenth century and so highly characteristic of it? Partly, perhaps, but also it may be the implicit conviction that there are no new plots, no primary stories left, only the possibility of repeating others. The sons are not free of the fathers but bound to the retracing of their traces. But yet again, the impossibility of original story, the need to retell, places the primary emphasis of the tale on the plane of narration itself, calls attention to the attempt to repeat, reconstruct, retell. In the act of narration, the narrators often end up telling a different story from that they imagined they were telling: the narrator of *The Aspern Papers,* for instance, tells the story of his own crime while intending to tell that of a detection. Marlow, thinking to tell us of Kurtz's victory wrested from innumerable defeats, himself wrests a kind of defeat from the postulated victory.

But to state the outcome of *Heart of Darkness* as either victory or defeat is to posit for it a finality which its very form subverts. In an essay on Henry James, Conrad talks about conventional novelistic ends, what he calls "the usual methods of solution by rewards and punishments, by crowned love, by fortune, by a broken leg or a sudden death." He goes on to note: "These solutions are legitimate inasmuch as they satisfy the desire for finality, for which our hearts yearn, with a longing greater than the longing for the loaves and the fishes of this earth. Perhaps the only true desire of mankind, coming thus to light in its hours of leisure, is to be set at rest." Thus does Conrad offer his version of *Beyond the Pleasure Principle*. That the challenging storyteller should refuse this "rest," postpone and defer the quiescence of the end, becomes clear as Conrad goes on to characterize James's nonfinal, rest-less endings: "You remain with the sense of the life still going on; and even the subtle presence of the dead is felt in that silence that comes upon the artist-creation when the last word has been read." The presence of the dead: certain ghosts, such as Kurtz's, are never laid to rest. The effort to narrate one's life story as it relates to their numinous and baleful presence is never done. One must tell and tell again, hoping that one's repetition will in turn be repeated, that one's voice will re-echo.

Forceful Overhearing

Aaron Fogel

Forceful overhearing is the condition in which Conrad places himself toward English, the condition in which he wants to place the reader vis-à-vis his writing, and the condition in which he often situates his most convincing characters. To make an incomplete list of Conrad's overhearers as dramatic figures: Stevie, the reduced Pentheus in *The Secret Agent,* overhears polemical talk and overreacts, while his over-protective sister, Winnie, herself participates as overreactive over-hearer, as has already been discussed. Razumov in *Under Western Eyes,* in many respects the climactic figure in the development of the theme of overhearing in Conrad's work, stands as the world's over-hearer. Once Haldin has made him his involuntary confessor, Razumov goes on to become an unwilling listening spy among Geneva's utopian revolutionaries. Marlow overhears savage yells and describes himself as being almost seduced by them; he also overhears tele-graphic conspiratorial talk and becomes obsessed with Kurtz as a voice. In a strong scene early in *Lord Jim,* the friendship of Jim and Marlow starts when Jim overreacts to the phrase "wretched cur," which he mistakenly thinks was spoken by Marlow about him; Jim's overreacting pride and amplification of the phrase make him acces-sible and extremely likable for perhaps the first time in the book. Davidson in the bitterly entitled "Because of the Dollars" is over-heard by the thieves, who used the information to rob Laughing

From *Coercion to Speak: Conrad's Poetics of Dialogue.* © 1985 by the President and Fellows of Harvard College. Harvard University Press, 1985.

Anne, whose murder he later overhears helplessly in the darkness; overhearing is both cause and effect in that story. Heyst in *Victory* renounces his "taste for silence" when he is drawn, very strangely for him, to a noisy concert at Schomberg's, where Lena's voice seduces him. Navigating blind, Whalley in "The End of the Tether" can be said to be overhearing the sea in his last months, steering by overhearing and by talk with his Serang. Amy Foster is an "overhearer," an exaggerator of noises, whose hypersensitivity amplifies cries for help to the degree that she cannot stand them and runs away. "Sympathy" in that portrait becomes ironically identified with "*over*-hearing": the ability to be "sensitive" to cries is at the same time the cause of flight, which is why sympathy as a faculty, identified with the pathos of overhearing (as it is also for Winnie) is inactive and self-contradictory. Many of Conrad's ships seem designed as spaces of unavoidable overhearing. Hirsch dies for the disproportion between what he has and has not overheard. Marlow, Razumov, Stevie, Winnie, Heyst, Hirsch—among others—overhear the world involuntarily, amplifying, hearing one-sidedly and distortedly, so that moments in which they are "made to hear" define them and obligate them against their will; an overhearing is one of the determining and catastrophic events in their lives.

As this list should suggest, the scene of forced overhearing in Conrad is often marked by overreaction, and this kind of *over*hearing is not merely a device in his work but, like coercion to speak, is a theme. The literary background for this meaning of the scene of hypersensitive overhearing lies also in the tragic tradition, as when Greek choruses are passively horrified by cries from the household, or most saliently, as when Polonius overreacts to the quarrel between Hamlet and Gertrude. Whatever real violence there is between the mother and the son, Polonius is an instance of hyperbole by the eavesdropper, indicated as the likely result of the position of overhearing. Shakespeare of course not infrequently seems to go almost inadvertently to the heart of a particular dialogue form while apparently exploiting it only for the action; in the arras scene he manages to suggest that the essence of the scene of overhearing is unstable amplification, and that this is a political fact. Polonius crying out expresses the ignorance and overreaction inherent in the overhearer's position, which flattens the sense of relation and context felt by the speakers themselves, and thereby, oddly enough, unrealistically amplifies the force of what they say.

Mikhail Bakhtin, in a sketch of "the history of laughter," argues that the scene of overhearing—without the double meaning I have just given it—lies at the heart of bourgeois chamber comedy, and is linked to middle-class architecture and privacy: "Seventeenth century literature with its dialogue was a preparation to the 'alcove realism' of private life, a realism of eavesdropping and peeping which reached its climax in the nineteenth century." But in considering Conrad's new overhearers, Shakespeare's poetics of overhearing as amplification and Bakhtin's historical treatment of middle-class chamber comedy overhearing can serve only as first steps in placing his historical revision and interpretation of the scene. He makes it a new pathos. The overhearer in Conrad, often the central figure, does not listen in or spy intentionally, but is forced to hear, situated as the overhearer against his own will. Winnie, Stevie, Razumov, and Heyst may be the most powerful examples of this kind of victim of undesired information. As with the structure of coercion to speak, the structure of forcible overhearing appears on all levels: in Conrad's way of hearing words, in his picture of his own audience as made up of unwilling overhearers, and in his representations of modern persons as besieged by information.

"I doubt the heroism of the hearers," Conrad wrote in his essay on James, implying through one of his small prose chimes that audiences in general cannot be expected to make heroic efforts to understand difficulty novels, such as James's late work. The same chime (hero-hearer) applies to some of Conrad's own characters. His hearers, his heroes and heroines, have a heroism which is not absent, or simply negated, but rather continually "in doubt." We might take a fall from the high idea of the tragic overreacher, and say that in Conrad we have the tragic overhearer—like Winnie or Razumov—a character offered as typical of the modern era of disproportioning colonial relations, languages in contact, and forced information. This figure is neither as degraded as Polonius nor as safely situated in the alcove as Bakhtin's middle-class overhearer in farces and melodramas.

When, for example, Marlow in *Heart of Darkness* travels upriver, he finds himself in scenes of forced dialogue and involuntary overhearing. These are, in a disturbing way, both outdoor and indoor, international and domestic. They recreate what used to appear in tragic overhearings—a disturbing fusion of public and private for something beyond snooping and intrigue. At first, for example,

when at the beginning of part 2 he hears the manager talk and con-
spire about Kurtz, we feel it may be only part of an "adventure"; but
the main point soon becomes that everything in the closeness of the
Central Station brings Marlow into moral proximity with them. His
situation of overhearing them is not incidental but thematic. As in
tragedy, it sustains the sense that overhearing is bound up with evil
and with being "overwhelmed." This is part of the dialogue that he
overhears:

> "Anything since then?" asked the other hoarsely. "Ivory,"
> jerked the nephew: "lots of it—prime sort—lots—most
> annoying, from him." "And with that?" questioned the
> heavy rumble. "Invoice," was the reply fired out, so to
> speak. Then silence. They had been talking about Kurtz.

This is the moment in which two key terms, *Ivory*—the narrative
fetish—and *Invoice*—a poetic name for Marlow's growing obsession
with Kurtz's voice and his sense of obligation and debt vaguely associated with Kurtz—are brought together into an overheard and
overdetermined chiming parallelism. The polysemous word *Invoice*
here means something roughly equivalent to "inscape" in Hopkins,
but the force is more political and moral. Marlow from this point
onward goes mad with "Invoice" as the world is mad with "Ivory."
The scene goes beyond the "realism of eavesdropping and peeping"
described by Bakhtin to suggest that moments of overhearing—here
called moments of "Invoice"—in the context of modern colonialism,
are no longer funny, as in chamber comedy, or thrilling, but intolerable, maddening, nauseating. The overhearer is not primarily a spy
but a victim of what he hears. The setting thus is one of overhearing
as conspiratorial colonial drama; and the diction calls for the reader
also to "overhear" an odd prose chime, to be aurally hyperacute.

Having established that conspiratorial overhearing has an un-
usual force to rob the immersed listener of his moral autonomy ("Invoice"), Conrad goes on to objectify overhearing further in *Heart of
Darkness*. In a later scene, Marlow and the "pilgrims" find themselves blinded with a dense opaque mist, and suddenly overhear native threat/lamentations. Overhearing, in both senses, now dramatizes not domestic space, and not conspiracy, but simply and starkly
the relation between alien peoples. This is reinforced by the way in
which the wall is not architectural but natural, a wall of mist. This
stark relation is not one of "Invoice" of the moral sort, personal ob-

ligation or obsession, but an objective wall, which seems to Marlow's aural imagination itself to speak about its own existence. "To me it seemed as though the mist itself had screamed," Marlow says. The wall of mist, as a white darkness, or a "blind whiteness," obviously and deliberately comprises the moral blindness of the white race, and also combines the two "races," white and black, light and darkness, into a single whole, as will the action of the story: a case in which Conrad might fairly be said to be undoing the simplistic opposition between the races by a natural image. This white darkness itself seems to cry out, even while it is itself the barrier and the protective wall between the peoples. Conrad here tries, in another example of fusion, to turn the "comic" and "scheming" conventions of overhearing inside out. The wall itself speaks. To Marlow's hypersensitive imagination, it prevents itself as a natural barrier that "objects to" itself: that is, it points out its own objectivity at the same time that it protests against its own existence. This occurs only ten pages after the more conspiratorial scene of overhearing at the start of part 2. The scene of overhearing here is theme, not device; its structure is violently foregrounded, and it is given a shifting historical meaning. Overhearing now speaks out overloudly against itself. The amplification of overhearing becomes the emblematic condition of languages in contact and peoples in contact. The scene is *not* what might be called romantic bathos; on the contrary, it is an attempt to undo that bathos—the poetry of the desperate cry—by resetting it historically. "Romanticism," for Conrad, is the literary expression of imperialism in its dialogical disproportions. Its "overheardnesses," its half dialogues, its longings, cries, ambiguous speech acts, and prophecies, even its sense of adventure, grow out of the dramatic conditions of colonialism. The scene of the absolute mist that seems itself to scream is an attempt to picture the historical self-contradictions of romanticism objectively.

Let us go back for a moment and consider the glossary of Conrad's poetic terms I have been accumulating slowly here: "detonation" as a pun that "explodes" the dialectic of sound and silence; "impression" as historically polysemous and reminding us of force in dialogue; Lingard as lingering guardianship, or the temporizing of colonialism; the physical but also social triad rest, unrest, arrest, whose importance to the construction of Conrad's scenes I have only suggested; Invoice-Ivory as one of the points of welding between dialogic obsession and narrative fetish in *Heart of Darkness;* must-

muster as the modern scene of hiring; hero-hearer; ough-cough. Each of these is deployed, in the readings I have given, for the creation of dramatic and representational ideas. What may be difficult for most readers now to accept is that the device of prose rhyme here, which we are accustomed to think of as only hermetic or abstract, is put in the service of his moral and historical imagination, and in all seriousness. I would go so far as to say that Conrad at many high points in his work *thinks in* what he would probably call either "chimes" or "accords" (we would be likely to call them prose rhymes or prose off rhymes). These are among his most important ideas, and they are generated as a response to the historical and personal condition of being an overhearer of English. He invents a poetics of overhearing which comprises both diction and scene construction. Author, readers, and characters are united in a condition of overhearing, which generates a different kind of vocabulary. This in turn is part of his most characteristic idiosyncrasy as a fiction writer, which is to create unexpected "poetic" fusions between the narrative and the dialogical structures with which he works. For example, Ivory, which is the colonial fetish, chimes jarringly with Invoice, which is one term for Marlow's moral obsession with Kurtz's voice. The general effect of this kind of structure is to insist that dialogue forms are inseparably and forcefully fused to narrative events. The two—dialogue and narrative—do not so much alternate or support one another as "fuse" violently and try to take each other over. Chimes or accords are among the instruments, or "rivets," by which Conrad holds our idea of the narrative action of any story to the idea of the dialogic of that story. As a result, the argument as to whether Conrad is a literalist or a deconstructionist becomes itself somewhat shallow. What he is is a writer who fuses dialogue and narrative in such a way that each seems to seek domination over the other. This is not deconstruction but the presentation of a world of force, in which even those abstract ingredients, dialogue and narrative, try to force each other into subordination, try to conquer each other, like imperial powers; and this amounts to a bizarre subversion of the hybrid nature of the novel itself, which usually either seeks to blend dialogue to narrative harmoniously or to joke in various entertaining ways about their disharmony and mutual interruption.

The sense of a delicate balance of forces between persons can also be felt throughout his letters. Commentary on the letters has paid attention mainly to his ideas or to data about his life. I would

like here to pay some attention to his epistolary ways of saying
"you." If there is a keynote phrase for *Heart of Darkness,* from this
standpoint, it is not "the horror!" but the phrase "you,—even you!"
which appears in a famous letter to Robert Cunninghame Graham.
Graham had just highly praised part 1 of the story. Conrad's long
answer to this praise is written in alternating French and English
stripes. He quarrels with Graham's socialist optimism and pacifism,
describes society as organized criminality, and condemns everything
Russian. Though later passages are more often quoted, for present
purposes the opening of the letter is especially interesting:

> I am simply in seventh heaven to find you like the "H. of
> D." so far. You bless me indeed. Mind you don't curse me
> by and bye for the very same thing. There are two more
> instalments in which the idea is so wrapped up in second-
> ary notions that you,—even you!—may miss it. And also
> you must remember that I don't start with an abstract no-
> tion. I start with definite images and as their rendering is
> true some little effect is produced. So far the note struck
> chimes in with your convictions,—*mais après?* There is an
> *après.* But I think that if you look a little into the episodes,
> you will find in them the right intention, though I fear
> nothing that is practically effective.
>
> *Somme toute, c'est une bête d'histoire qui aurait pu être quel-
> que chose de très bien si j'avais su l'écrire.*
>
> The thing on West. Gar. is excellent, excellent. I am
> most interested in your plans of work and travel. I don't
> know in which most. *Nous allons causer de tout cela.*

The striping of French and English goes on in other letters, of
course. It has an odd quality that might be variously called affecta-
tion, sheer frustration with language, split personality, Polishness,
or dialogism. Consider the last possibility. The two languages here
correspond to two slightly different attitudes toward dialogue. The
French Conrad—throughout the rest of the well-known letter too
long to quote here—articulates a Balzacian theory of society as organized crime, and paints a Vautrin-like picture of universal criminality; it leads him to imply that all order is therefore arbitrary, not
just, and that anyone who affirms order must not try to affirm it as
natural. The English Conrad is more personal and less bitter. He
relies on direct address of his friend, and on a play of richly allusive

"speech acts"—a primary English mannerism long before Austin
analyzed it—to continually achieve social "touch." He sounds less
skeptical, more local and communal. "You bless me . . . mind you
don't curse me by and bye." In French he calls chat *causerie,* a word
which derives from the legal pleading of causes, which as in *Bleak
House* goes on endlessly: "Nous allons causer de tout cela." Thus, in
French, "conversation," chatting, is oddly if obliquely and gently
linked to causality, ideology, and legal debate. But English leads
Conrad to make his dialogue with Graham a sympathetic musical
connection, less legalistic, more irrational, and at the same time
more modest, a villager's model: "So far the note struck chimes in
with your convictions." The common but not clichéd phrasal verb
"chimes in with" is highly characteristic of Conrad's English at this
period. It is arguably more vivid and local than the French equivalent, *accord.* In keeping with the metaphor of chiming, which is one
of Conrad's key metaphors for relations between persons, the
strongest chime in the letter itself is the chiming phrase "you,—even
you!" While this seems to be flattery—even someone as attentive and
sympathetic to me as you will have trouble with my increasingly
dark story—the ultimate burden of the whole letter, addressed in
aggressive critical friendship to Graham, is unflattering and critical.
It is, we'd have to say, a letter of I and You. Graham himself—even
Graham—is one of us criminal animals with a capricious will to destroy—a *frondeur* Conrad calls him—and the world is a place of *bêtise. Heart of Darkness* itself is *une bête d'histoire,* a stupid story, and the
clearest "secondary" message of the story will not be "the horror!"
but a feeling of universal *bêtise:* "you,—even you!" addressed to
Marlow, to Graham as liberal socialist, and to the reader. If we want
to feel Conrad's linguistic precision here, his exploitation of the gaps
between languages, we can point not only to the gap between *accord*
in French (which is rational-harmonic) and "chimes in with" (which
is local, idiomatic, and perhaps Dickensian) but also to the gap between *une bête d'histore* and "a beastly story."

It seems willful to make "you,—even you!" a keynote for *Heart
of Darkness,* when the phrase occurs not in the story but in a letter to
Graham. Yet in fact a good case can be made that the writing down
of the Congo experience was catalyzed precisely by Conrad's reading
of *Mogreb-el-Acksa,* Graham's account of his travels in Morocco, and
that to some degree Conrad's famous story was a reply to, a dialogue
with, and finally a refutation of his flamboyant friend. The charac-

teristic sentence of *Mogreb-el-Acksa,* much like its plot, travels freely, through a combination of events, folklore, and philosophical reflections, to end up nowhere; it is long, apparently semidirectionless, but stylistically alert, full of commas, Byronic, with a little more meander than punch. A frontispiece map to the travelogue shows the main plot, the failed attempt to reach the mysterious city of Tarudant, so that the journey's dotted line loops back onto itself to make a big lasso to the north of the goal. Graham's writing is singularly entertaining, and Conrad, just before he probably began work on *Heart of Darkness*—written rapidly—praised it with real and unforced enthusiasm in letters to both Graham and Graham's mother. One can see why. Yet Graham's vivid and appealing style is antithetical to Conrad's own. Marlow is a kind of Graham stunned into afterthought and tragic direction. The plot of Conrad's story, in spite of Conrad's insistence (to Graham, whose work he was stealing and refuting) in the letter above that "I don't start with an abstract notion" in fact does abstract—though on the basis of real experience— the journey of Graham's free loop. Marlow is confined to a river. The strong linearity of his trip abstracts the freer, less narrow journey of the freebooter Graham, just as everything in Conrad's style in the story *swings to,* that is, has a compelled or tethered directionality. Graham's swashbuckling, freebooting, filibustering style of travel and writing masterfully combines vanity and diffidence and Shavian moralizing; he becomes, in Conrad's brutally addressive story, Marlow, "you,—even you!" the domineering but likable yarn spinner made to hear his own flowing periods as compulsivity rather than freedom. Having read and probably loved the zany folklorist voice of *Mogreb-el-Acksa,* Conrad used his own radically more involuntary political experience to steal and correct Graham's "plot," in which the hero, almost happily, never reaches the dark goal of his travels. Conrad's story takes the key prepositional mood, "to," which is the force of both stories, and makes it a matter of compulsion more than roving will; in addition, he makes it forcefully interpersonal and addressive. The effect is to become his main organizational gesture: that of turning someone else's apparently "free" text into a more coerced action, all within the hidden dialogue of answering someone else's deludedly free account of events.

There was no demonic bitterness in this. Conrad seems personally to have taken real pleasure in the freedoms of other people's styles. But in his writing he always found himself critically reconstructing those freedoms to make stories which display—grace-fully—a more coercive reality: not so much a determining Nature as persons coercing other persons in a plurality of ways. This was no narrow impulse to see slavery everywhere but the result of historical experiences he could not alter. His personal good humor can be seen at times in the letters. A small sentence from one of them is worth looking at, though perhaps no other critic would. Edward Garnett had been dangerously ill and was recovering. He had some of the manuscript of the book then called *The Rescuer;* Conrad expressed joy about the recovery, and then wrote, "Don't you read the *Resc.;* read nothing but Rabelais, if you must read." The sentence is in a mock-imperative mood, exuberant, friendly, and playful. His advice to read Rabelais may not seem like one of the key moments in the letters, but is startling if we want to dwell on his grimness rather than his dialogism. He implies here that his own work would be less healthy for a convalescent than Rabelais. And he jokes, typically and colloquially, that reading is experienced in the mood of "must." But most interesting is the spontaneous transformation of sounds in the first phrase. The potentially plain, self-conscious, and stern sentence "Don't read *The Rescuer*" is transformed into the energetically dial-ogized "Don't you read the *Resc.*" Unconsciously, naturally, he ab-breviates, contracts, foreshortens the title of his own work, drop-ping the sound "you" in that word to transpose it to the idiomatic and friendly "Don't you read." The gesture, entirely unconscious, entirely sincere, is therefore that of erasing his own command of the "you" in "rescue." His own "rescuer" powers in the melancholy book *The Rescuer* are disavowed: *The Rescuer* would not rescue you now in your convalescence: Rabelais would be healthier stuff. "Res-cue" is given back to "you." The little sentence is not mainly a con-demnation of his own work as morbid; it implies instead a sane per-spective on himself, and on the effects of his writing on others. The modest sentence in its friendly, transposed "you" sound is one unaf-fected and spontaneous example of his feeling for the dialogical placement of echoes in prose. When Kurtz says, "The horror!" twice, it's narcissism: even in his most "curt" moment, he can't stop the histrionic self-chiming. At the moment of last resort, he falls into selfishly penitential repetition. It is, probably, a final joke about his egoism. Conrad, unlike Kurtz, whom he was afraid he resembled, and despite limits and tautnesses, had the strongest possible dra-matic awareness of the presence and absence of the "you" in acts of "rescue."

Chronology

1857	Józef Teodor Konrad Korzeniowski born December 3, in Berdyczew, Poland, to Apollo Korzeniowski and Ewelina Bobrowska.
1862	Apollo Korzeniowski is exiled to Russia for his part in the Polish National Committee. His wife and son accompany him.
1865	Conrad's mother dies.
1869	Apollo Korzeniowski and son return to Cracow in February. Apollo dies on May 23.
1874	Conrad leaves Cracow for Marseilles, intending to become a sailor.
1875	Conrad is an apprentice aboard the *Mont Blanc,* bound for Martinique.
1877	Conrad is part owner of the *Tremolino,* which carries illegal arms to the Spanish pretender, Don Carlos.
1878	In February, after ending an unhappy love affair, Conrad attempts suicide by shooting himself. In June, he lands in England. He serves as ordinary seaman on the *Mavis.*
1883	Becomes mate on the ship *Riversdale.*
1884	Is second mate on the *Narcissus,* bound from Bombay to Dunkirk.
1886	Conrad becomes a naturalized British citizen.
1887	Is first mate on the *Highland Forest.*
1889	Begins writing *Almayer's Folly.*
1890	In May, Conrad leaves for the Congo as second in command of the S.S. *Roi de Belges,* later becoming commander.
1894	On January 14, he ends his sea career.

1895	Publishes *Almayer's Folly.* Writes *An Outcast of the Islands.* He is now living in London.
1896	Conrad marries Jessie George on March 24.
1897–1900	Writes *The Nigger of the "Narcissus," Heart of Darkness,* and *Lord Jim.*
1904	Completes *Nostromo.*
1905	Granted Civil List Pension. Travels in Europe for four months.
1907	Writes *The Secret Agent.*
1911–12	Writes *Under Western Eyes* and *'Twixt Land and Sea.*
1914	Writes *Chance* and *Victory.* In July, Conrad visits Poland, where he is caught when the Great War breaks out on August 4. He escapes and returns safely to England in November.
1916	Conrad's son, Borys, is fighting on the French front.
1917	Writes *The Shadow-Line* and prefaces to an edition of his collected works.
1918	Armistice, November 11.
1919	Conrad writes *The Arrow of Gold.* He moves to Oswalds, Bishopsbourne, near Canterbury, where he spends his last years.
1920	Writes *The Rescue.*
1924	In May, Conrad declines a knighthood. After an illness, he dies of a heart attack on August 3 and is buried in Canterbury.
1925	The incomplete *Suspense* is published. *Tales of Hearsay* is published.
1926	*Last Essays* published.

Contributors

HAROLD BLOOM, Sterling Professor of the Humanities at Yale University, is the author of *The Anxiety of Influence, Poetry and Repression*, and many other volumes of literary criticism. His forthcoming study, *Freud: Transference and Authority*, attempts a full-scale reading of all of Freud's major writings. A MacArthur Prize Fellow, he is general editor of five series of literary criticism published by Chelsea House.

ALBERT J. GUERARD is the author of *Conrad the Novelist* and *The Triumph of the Novel: Dickens, Dostoyevsky, and Faulkner*. He is Professor of English at Stanford University.

JAMES GUETTI is Professor of English at Rutgers University.

C. B. COX is Professor of English at the University of Manchester, England, and the author of *The Free Spirit: A Study of Liberal Humanism* and an edition of critical essays on Shakespeare.

BRUCE HENRICKSEN teaches English at Loyola University.

R. A. GEKOSKI is the author of *Conrad: The Moral World of the Novelist*.

IAN WATT is Professor of English at Stanford University and the author of *Conrad in the Nineteenth Century* and *The Rise of the Novel: Studies in Defoe, Richardson, and Fielding*.

JOHN TESSITORE is a Fellow at the State University of New York, Stony Brook, and has published both poetry and critical essays.

PETER BROOKS is Tripp Professor of the Humanities at Yale. He is the author of *The Novel of Worldliness*, *The Melodramatic Imagination*, and *Reading for the Plot*.

AARON FOGEL teaches English at Boston University.

Bibliography

Baines, Jocelyn. *Joseph Conrad: A Critical Biography.* New York: McGraw-Hill, 1960.

Beach, Joseph Warren. "Impressionism: Conrad." In *The Twentieth Century Novel: Studies in Technique,* 337–65. New York: Appleton-Century, 1932.

Berman, Jeffrey. *Joseph Conrad: Writing as Rescue.* New York: Astra, 1977.

Blackmur, R. P. *Eleven Essays in the European Novel.* New York: Harbinger, 1954.

Bradbrook, M. C. *Joseph Conrad: Poland's English Genius.* Cambridge: Cambridge University Press, 1941.

Brown, Robert. "Integrity and Self-Deception." *The Critical Review* 25 (1983): 115–31.

Conradiana: A Journal of Joseph Conrad, 1968–.

Crews, Frederick. "The Power of Darkness." *Partisan Review* 34 (1967): 507–25.

Daiches, David. *The Novel and the Modern World.* Chicago: University of Chicago Press, 1960.

Daleski, H. M. *Joseph Conrad: The Way of Dispossession.* London: Faber & Faber, 1977.

Ehrsam, T. G. *A Bibliography of Conrad.* Metuchen, N.J.: Scarecrow, 1969.

Ellis, James. "Kurtz's Voice: The Intended as 'The Horror.'" *English Literature in Transition* 19 (1976): 105–10.

Ellman, Richard, and Charles Feidelson, eds. *The Modern Tradition.* New York: Oxford University Press, 1965.

Evans, Robert O. "Conrad's Underworld." *Modern Fiction Studies* 2 (May 1956): 56–62.

Fogel, Aaron. *Coercion to Speak: Conrad's Poetics of Dialogue.* Cambridge: Harvard University Press, 1965.

Frye, Northrop. *Anatomy of Criticism.* Princeton: Princeton University Press, 1957.

Gillon, Adam. *The Eternal Solitary.* New York: Bookman, 1960.

———. *Joseph Conrad.* Boston: Twayne, 1982.

Gillon, Adam, and Ludwik Krzyanowski, eds. *Joseph Conrad: Commemorative Essays.* New York: Astra, 1975.

Glassman, Peter J. *Language and Being: Joseph Conrad and the Literature of Personality.* New York: Columbia University Press, 1976.

Guerard, Albert J. *Conrad the Novelist.* Cambridge: Harvard University Press, 1958.

———. *Joseph Conrad.* New York: New Directions, 1947.

Harkness, Bruce, ed. *Conrad's* Heart of Darkness *and the Critics*. Belmont, Calif.: Wadsworth, 1960.

Hawkins, Hunt. "Conrad's Critique of Imperialism in *Heart of Darkness.*" *PMLA* 94 (1979): 286–99.

Johnson, Bruce M. *Conrad's Models of Mind*. Minneapolis: University of Minnesota Press, 1971.

Joseph Conrad Today: The Newsletter of the Joseph Conrad Society of America, 1975–.

Kirschner, Robert. *Heart of Darkness: The Psychologist as Artist*. Edinburgh: Oliver & Boyd, 1968.

Krupat, Arnold. "Antonymy, Language, and Value in Conrad's *Heart of Darkness.*" *The Missouri Review* 3, no. 1 (1979): 63–85.

Kulkarni, H. B. "Buddhistic Structure and Significance in *Heart of Darkness.*" *South Asian Review* 3 (1979):67–75.

Leavis, F. R. *The Great Tradition: George Eliot, Henry James, Joseph Conrad*. New York: New York University Press, 1963.

Levin, Gerald. "Victorian Kurtz." *Journal of Modern Literature* 7 (1979): 433–40.

McLauchlan, Juliet. "The 'Value' and 'Significance' of *Heart of Darkness.*" *Conradian* 15 (1983): 3–21.

Meisel, Perry. "Decentering Heart of Darkness." *Modern Language Studies* 8, no. 3 (1978): 20–28.

Meyer, Bernard C. *Joseph Conrad: A Psychoanalytic Biography*. Princeton: Princeton University Press, 1967.

Miller, J. Hillis. *Poets of Reality: Six Twentieth Century Writers*. New York: Atheneum, 1969.

Mudrick, Marvin, ed. *Conrad: A Collection of Critical Essays*. Englewood Cliffs, N.J.: Prentice-Hall, 1966.

Ong, Walter J., S. J. "Truth in Conrad's Darkness." *Mosaic* 11, no. 1 (1977): 151–63.

Palmer, John A. *Joseph Conrad's Fiction: A Study in Literary Growth*. Ithaca, N.Y.: Cornell University Press, 1968.

Parry, Benita. *Conrad's Imperialism*. Englewood Cliffs, N.J.: Salem, 1984.

Renner, Stanley. "Kurtz, Christ, and the Darkness of *Heart of Darkness.*" *Renascence* 28 (1976): 95–104.

Roussel, Royal. *The Metaphysics of Darkness*. Baltimore: Johns Hopkins University Press, 1971.

Said, Edward W. *Joseph Conrad and the Fiction of Autobiography*. Cambridge: Harvard University Press, 1966.

Sams, Larry Marshall. "*Heart of Darkness:* The Meaning around the Nutshell." *International Fiction Review* 5 (1978): 129–33.

Stallman, Robert W., ed. *The Art of Joseph Conrad: A Critical Symposium*. East Lansing: Michigan State University Press, 1960.

Steiner, Joan E. "Modern Pharisees and False Apostles: Ironic New Testament Parallels in Conrad's *Heart of Darkness.*" *Nineteenth-Century Fiction* 37 (1982): 75–96.

Steward, Garrett. "Lying as Dying in *Heart of Darkness.*" *PLMA* 95 (1980): 319–31.

Tennant, Roger. *Joseph Conrad: A Biography*. New York: Atheneum, 1981.

Thornburn, David. *Conrad's Romanticism*. New Haven: Yale University Press, 1974.

Thumbo, Edwin. "Some Plain Reading: Marlow's Lie in *Heart of Darkness.*" *The Literary Criterion* 16, no. 3 (1981): 12–22.

Verleun, Jan. "Conrad's *Heart of Darkness:* Marlow and the Intended." *Neophilolgus* 67 (1983): 621–39.

Watt, Ian. "Marlow, Henry James, and *Heart of Darkness.*" *Nineteenth-Century Fiction* 33 (1978): 159–74.

―――. *Conrad in the Nineteenth Century.* Berkeley: University of California Press, 1979.

Watts, Cedric. *Conrad's* Heart of Darkness: *A Critical and Contextual Discussion.* Milan, Italy: Mursia International, 1977.

Whitehead, Lee M. "Recent Conrad Criticism." *Dalhousie Review* 61 (1981–82): 743–49.

Zak, William. "Conrad, F. R. Leavis, and Whitehead: *Heart of Darkness* and Organic Holism." *Conradiana* 4 (1972): 5–24.

Acknowledgments

"The Journey Within" by Albert J. Guerard from *Conrad the Novelist* by Albert J. Guerard, © 1986 by Albert J. Guerard. Reprinted by permission of the author and Harvard University Press.

"*Heart of Darkness:* The Failure of Imagination" by James Guetti from *The Limits of Metaphor* by James Guetti. This essay originally appeared in *The Sewanee Review* 73, no. 3 (Summer 1965), © 1965 by the University of the South. Reprinted by permission of the editor of *The Sewanee Review.*

"*Heart of Darkness:* A Choice of Nightmares?" by C. B. Cox from *Joseph Conrad: The Modern Imagination* by C. B. Cox, © 1974 by C. B. Cox. Reprinted by permission of the author and Rowman & Littlefield, Totowa, New Jersey, and J. M. Dent & Sons Ltd. Publishers.

"*Heart of Darkness* and the Gnostic Myth" by Bruce Henricksen from *Mosaic* 11, no. 4 (Summer 1978), © 1978 by the University of Manitoba Press. Reprinted by permission.

"*Heart of Darkness*" by R. A. Gekoski from *Conrad: The Moral World of the Novelist* by R. A. Gekoski, © 1978 by R. A. Gekoski. Reprinted by permission of Harper & Row Publishers.

"*Heart of Darkness* and Nineteenth-Century Thought" by Ian Watt from *Partisan Review* 45, no. 1 (1978), © 1978 by Ian Watt. Reprinted by permission of the author and *Partisan Review.*

"Freud, Conrad, and *Heart of Darkness*" by John Tessitore from *College Literature* 7, no. 1 (1980), © 1980 by West Chester University. Reprinted by permission.

"An Unreadable Report: Conrad's *Heart of Darkness*" by Peter Brooks from *Reading for the Plot: Design and Intention in Narrative* by Peter Brooks, © 1984 by Peter Brooks. Reprinted by permission of Alfred A. Knopf, Inc.

"Forceful Overhearing" (originally entitled "Dialogue and Labor") by Aaron Fogel from *Coercion to Speak: Conrad's Poetics of Dialogue* by Aaron Fogel, © 1985 by the President and Fellows of Harvard College. Reprinted by permission of Harvard University Press.

Index